Prudence Crandall

Prudence Crandall

AN INCIDENT OF RACISM IN

NINETEENTH-CENTURY CONNECTICUT

By EDMUND FULLER

WESLEYAN UNIVERSITY PRESS

Middletown, Connecticut

ISBN: 0-8195-4030-7

Library of Congress Catalog Card Number: 71-120264

Manufactured in the United States of America

FIRST EDITION

In Memoriam
M. L. K.
R. F. K.

The question between us is not simply whether thirty or **forty** colored girls shall be well educated at a school to be kept in Canterbury; but whether the people in any part of our land will recognize and generously protect the "inalienable rights of man," without distinction of color.

. . . the *greatest* question our nation is now called upon to decide—i.e. whether our immense colored population shall henceforth be permitted to rise among us, *as they may be able,* in intellectual and moral worth; or be kept down in hopeless degradation, until in the providence of a just God they may throw off the yoke of their oppressors, with vindictive violence.

The spirit that is in the children of men is usually roused by persecution.

SAMUEL J. MAY

Contents

Illustrations

PRUDENCE CRANDALL

Preface

THIS BOOK TELLS ABOUT A LITTLE-KNOWN EPISODE IN THE village of Canterbury, Connecticut, in the years 1831–1834. When it happened it was seen to have national implications. Today also it has relevance to our immediate problems, at a time when tensions between blacks and whites often reach dangerous pitch. As a part of the historic background, what happened in Canterbury then is an aid to understanding what is happening now in the country at large.

Black militants may feel that there is nothing in this book for them, that they do not need it to support their charge that racism has always been present in American life. Nor are they interested in the fact that America has always had white people dedicated to fighting against injustice to blacks. But the struggle between Prudence Crandall and her respectable fellow townsmen has much to say to the present-day middle-class white man. He can see here how deeply ingrained racism is in our history, and how people otherwise of reasonable good will and unimpugned respectability could be trapped in passions of prejudice and stubbornness before they knew what had hit them. He can see also a community's capacity, in the passage of time, to come to its senses and repent its errors. But there will not always be time.

Many Americans have a vague impression that all race troubles over 150 years ago were specifically about slaves and were confined to the South. This story shows the problems of free blacks in the heart of a state that even then believed itself to be the paragon of the enlightened liberal North. Samuel J. May, one of the principal actors, wrote in the midst of this drama, in 1833, that "we have long since perceived how deep and inveterate, even in New England, are the prejudices of the whites against those of African descent."

It is not only more than a local, but also something more than a race story, showing forth as it does many facets of the New England reform spirit and diverse persons touched by it.

The story has been told a number of times, in obscure old pamphlets, scholarly quarterlies, and once in a sentimentalized, fictionalized version for young readers. It has not been told before in anything approaching the completeness of this account, with a look at so many of its ramifications, a probing of its cast of characters, and addressed to general readers.

I stumbled upon the story of Prudence in the 1940's, while doing research for a novel, *A Star Pointed North,* based on the life of the ex-slave and Abolitionist leader Frederick Douglass, the first authentic Negro hero in American history. I wrote a brief article, "Prudence of Canterbury," which appeared in *The American Scholar* in the summer of 1949. In the following years I felt certain that I must return to the story again. I have read all I could find of both primary and secondary source materials, including handling some of the letters of Prudence Crandall's old age, and the faded, handwritten legal documents of her arrest and various trials, in the archives of the Connecticut State Library in Hartford.

By extending the story beyond the village where it happened, tracing its linkages and repercussions, looking briefly at the rest of the careers of people involved on both sides of it, and by showing the tide of events in the history of American black men of which it was a small part, examining even the roots of the village of Canterbury, I have tried to give my fellow white Americans, in particular, a new glimpse into our own past, which may add something to the way in which we think about the present, or think about ourselves. Some arguments and attitudes of Prudence's oppressors are still met today.

I have been as accurate as I could, seeking a balance where accounts vary. Small aspects of the tale are blurred or contradictory in the sources. As this book is for general readers I have not burdened it with close documentation. All statements of fact and conjecture are based on the materials named in the list of sources. Most important, no dialogue whatever has been invented by me—every quoted word comes from one or another of those records.

Though I admire Prudence Crandall and those who stood with her in her ordeal, I have attempted to tell the story with detachment and irony, not attributing saintliness to one side or depravity to the other. That is always the best hope of coming somewhere near the truth.

In a document quoted herein, free Negroes meeting in convention in Philadelphia, in 1817, expressed themselves as "not desirous of increasing their prosperity but by honest efforts, and by the use of those opportunities for their improvement, which the constitution and the laws allow to all." It is the betrayal of those expectations, and denial of those opportunities, from then until now, more than the fact that slavery once existed, that have brought to pass the racial bitterness and violence of the present time.

CHAPTER I

The Jail

O N THE MORNING OF SATURDAY, JUNE 27, 1833, A SHERIFF entered the most beautiful house on the village green of Canterbury, Connecticut, and arrested Miss Prudence Crandall, Quaker gentlewoman and schoolmistress. She was expecting him. Twenty-nine-year-old Prudence was taken before two Justices of the Peace, her fellow townsmen Rufus Adams and Asael Bacon.

The charge was that "with force and arms" she "willfully and knowingly did harbour and board certain coloured persons" who "were not inhabitants of any town in this state. . . ." She had no weapons and put up no fight. The phrase "with force and arms" was a standard formula of legal jargon; the accurate words would have been "with obstinate determination." She was defying Connecticut's so-called "Black Law," a statute passed only four weeks earlier by the Legislature in response to a petition from citizens of Canterbury, and directed specifically at Prudence Crandall, who had opened a school for colored girls in the heart of their town.

The arraignment did not take long. Prudence was committed to stand trial at the August session of the Superior Court, in nearby Brooklyn, Connecticut. Meanwhile, she would be jailed unless a bond were posted of at least $150—some accounts say $300. This was routine. Justices Adams and Bacon, and the sheriff, believed that they were simply setting in motion the convenient machinery which would eliminate a nuisance. But Prudence did not post the bond.

PRUDENCE CRANDALL. Portrait by Francis Alexander, 1834. Courtesy Cornell University Libraries; Photo Science Studios, Cornell University.

SAMUEL J. MAY. Courtesy Cornell University Libraries; Photo
Science Studios, Cornell University.

A young man was sent riding, at once, to the town of Brooklyn, six miles north of Canterbury, to seek the Reverend Samuel J. May, a Unitarian minister of that place, an Abolitionist known to approve of Miss Crandall's school for colored girls. The messenger told May what had happened, and that Prudence would go to jail unless he, or someone, gave bond.

Mr. May said that surely there must be gentlemen in Canterbury in a better position to give bond than he, so he would leave it to them. As May told it, the young man, disconcerted, said, "But are you not her friend?"

"Certainly, too sincerely her friend to give relief to her enemies in their present embarrassment: and I trust you will not find any one of her friends, or the patrons of her school, who will step forward to help them any more than myself."

"But, sir, do you mean to allow her to be put into jail?"

"Most certainly, if her persecutors are unwise enough to let such an outrage be committed."

The messenger rode back to the justices of Canterbury with his dismaying news. It was now past noon. The jail was in Brooklyn, and around 2:00 P.M. May received word that the sheriff was on his way from Canterbury, in a carriage, with Miss Crandall in custody. When they arrived, in the late afternoon, May, with a friend named George W. Benson and Benson's daughter Mary, was at the jail awaiting them.

Some of the Canterbury men who had instigated the arrest had accompanied the sheriff and his prisoner and now begged May and his friends to intervene and prevent the jailing. They had started a process they could not stop; they saw dimly the trap that was opening for them. They had not foreseen it, nor did they now have the resourcefulness to do the one thing that would prevent their public embarrassment—post bond for Miss Crandall themselves, even against her wishes.

May drew Prudence aside and, by his own account, addressed her privately, in what sounds to modern ears like the dialogue of melodrama: "If you now hesitate, if you dread the gloomy place so much as to wish to be saved from it, I will give bonds for you even now." He had the money in his pocket.

We can read her character in her answer: "O no, I am only afraid they will *not* put me into jail."

They went back to the sheriff and his party, who were shuffling about uncomfortably, hesitant to finish what they had come there to do. The lawmen stalled and debated among themselves.

The jail was small and not much used. Everyone knew that some two years earlier it had been occupied by a condemned murderer, one Oliver Watkins, who had strangled his wife with a whipcord, and was taken from the Brooklyn jail to his hanging.

Two of Prudence's enemies now approached May again. "It would be a damned shame"—May's account leaves blank spaces for the "damns"—"an eternal disgrace to the State, to have her put into jail, into the very room that Watkins had last occupied."

"Certainly, gentlemen, and you may prevent this, if you please."

But they protested, "We are not her friends; we are not in favor of her school: we don't want any more damned niggers coming among us. It is your place to stand by Miss Crandall and help her now. You and your damned abolition brethren have encouraged her to bring this nuisance into Canterbury, and it is damned mean in you to desert her now."

May said, "She knows we have not deserted her. . . . The law which her persecutors have persuaded our legislators to enact is an infamous one, worthy of the Dark Ages. It would be just as bad as it is, whether we should give bonds for her or not. But the people generally will not so soon realize how bad, how wicked, how cruel a law it is, unless we suffer her persecutors to inflict upon her all the penalties it prescribes. . . . If you see fit to keep her from imprisonment in the cell of a murderer for having proffered the blessing of a good education to those who, in our country, need it most, you may do so; *we shall not.*"

The men of Canterbury turned away, angry and cursing. There was further futile talk among them. Darkness was falling. It was around eight o'clock. The unhappy sheriff could stall no longer. Reluctantly he surrendered Prudence to the jailer. When she was locked in the cell, May bowed, as if in shame, and said grandiloquently: "The deed is done; completely done. It cannot be recalled. It has passed into the history of our nation and our age."

In fact the deed had been anticipated and elaborate preparations had been made. Prudence's Abolitionist counsellors understood well the manipulation of public effect. With the recent passage of the Black Law, her arrest had become inevitable. May and Benson had carefully approached all of Prudence's friends and sympathizers in the surrounding towns to make sure that no one of them innocently spoiled the situation by producing the bond. May then visited the jailer, an amiable man, arranged to have the cell thoroughly scrubbed out, and removed the old bed and mattress on which the murderer might once have slept.

Whether this ever was the murderer's cell was challenged by Prudence's opposition in a published "Statement of Facts." They claimed that "the cell referred to, is located in the opposite corner of the building. This statement is the only one, on this point, that has any claim to truth. Miss C. ought to have given herself a little trouble to correct those misstatements, in a public manner, and more especially to express, in some way or other, her acknowledgements for the gratuitous favors which she received at the hands of the Jailor. This was not done, however." Of course it was not. The effect had been shrewdly calculated.

Two beds were placed in the cell, one from May's house and one from Benson's. After the ritual of clanging the iron door shut upon Prudence, it was opened again and her friend Mary Benson was allowed to join her for the night. The next day, May and Benson posted the bond. Prudence and her voluntary cellmate left the jail. Prudence went back to the routine of her school. The odd, significant, and for too long relatively obscure case of Prudence Crandall, of Canterbury, Connecticut, was at midpoint in its course. A minor martyr had been made.

CHAPTER II

Prudence

THE DEMURE, DELICATE FLOWER CALLED QUAKER LADY IS NOT an apt image for the flesh-and-blood Quaker lady, Prudence Crandall. She was a strong, long-lasting bloom that did not easily wither or blight. Her portrait in oil, painted by Francis Alexander and long the property of Samuel J. May, now hangs in the Uris Library at Cornell University, together with one of May himself. Painted in the late stage of the crisis in Canterbury, it shows a face of great firmness, not beautiful but perhaps handsome, with just a hint of masculinity. She has a large mouth, mannish chin, prominent nose, and wide-set blue eyes. Her hair is worn a little severely, but no more so than was considered suitable for respectable gentlewomen of the period.

She was born on September 3, 1803, in Hopkinton, Rhode Island, thirty miles or so southwest of Providence. Her parents were Pardon Crandall and the former Esther Carpenter, whose mother's name had been Prudence and whose father's name was Hezekiah. Both names were passed along to Esther's children. The Crandalls led the austerely simple life of their faith, but like most of the New England Quakers after the early years of colonial persecution, they were comfortably prosperous, by inheritance and their own efforts, for Quakers were pre-eminently a self-respecting, frugal, hard-working lot, ant-like accumulators rather than grasshopper spendthrifts. Their spiritual life was most vulnerable, perhaps, to the conviction that also flourished in the minds of other New England puritans—that the prosperity of the faithful was God's reward for piety.

The tendency to get into controversy over matters of principle that later showed itself in Prudence had been seen early in the Crandall line. One John Crandall, in 1651, got himself arrested in Boston in a theological dispute with the orthodox Puritan theocracy over the proper view of baptism. After his release, he went to Rhode Island and helped to establish the community of Westerly, of which Hopkinton was an offshoot.

Pardon and Esther Crandall in 1810 sold their Hopkinton land, which had been a gift from her father, then recently deceased, and left Rhode Island. They didn't go far, but bought a farm in the little town of Canterbury, Connecticut. Their last child, Almira, was born there. They had four in all, Hezekiah, Prudence, and Reuben being the older ones.

Prudence had been educated at the Friends' Boarding School in Providence (known later as the Moses Brown School). It was superior schooling, as Quaker education has been consistently. We don't know the exact course of her life, but she surfaces, like her parents, in Connecticut, as a schoolteacher in Plainfield, a township near Canterbury but larger. Up to 1831 when she was twenty-seven, she was a stock type of the New England village, the Quaker spinster schoolmistress.

At that point the community of Canterbury happened to have a bumper crop of daughters of prominent families, just ripening to school age. To get instruction of the quality suitable to their class these girls would have to go afield, probably to board, for even a distance of ten miles or so was formidable in the horse-and-buggy era. Instead of sending the daughters of Canterbury away to school, why not bring school to their daughters?

There are disagreements about who made the first move for Prudence to open a school of her own. She was teaching in nearby Plainfield and was known in Canterbury, where her parents now lived. Some accounts say that the men who became

sponsors of her school sought her out and asked her to under-
take the project. Versions of those hostile to her, after the
trouble started, suggest that Prudence initiated the enterprise.
It is not worth arguing. What counts is that the school was
launched with enthusiasm all around.

A group of Canterbury's most prominent and wealthy citizens aided the venture. Some of these became the school's
"Board of Visitors," which is to say supervisors, overseers, or
trustees of a sort: State Attorney Andrew T. Judson; Dr. Andrew Harris, physician and surgeon, whose wife was the
daughter of General Moses Cleveland, a native of Canterbury,
for whom Cleveland, Ohio, is named; Daniel Frost, Jr., active
in the temperance movement; Rufus Adams, Justice of the
Peace, before whom Prudence was later arraigned; Samuel L.
Hough; William Kinne; Daniel Packer; and the Reverend
Dennis Platt. Several of these, most notably Judson, were close
neighbors of the school on the Green.

It was they who suggested and helped to procure for the
school a house that had been built in 1805* by Squire Elisha
Paine. Its latest owner, Luther Paine, had died recently. The
handsome house was, and still is, on the southwest corner of
the crossing of the principal roads, then called the Norwich
and Worcester, and Hartford and Providence, turnpikes—both
dirt roads, of course. Another corner house was Judson's.
Across the road from the school and a few hundred yards south
stood and still stands the Congregational church.

Some sources say that the sponsors helped Prudence raise
the funds to buy the property for the school. Precisely how
Prudence obtained her equity in it—whether she contributed
cash, whether it was in part a loan or gift—is not spelled out
anywhere. In any case, after the row began, she offered to sell
the property to her opponents and move her school to a less
conspicuous part of town.

---

* Or 1792 or 1815; there is evidence for all three of these dates. It was purchased in 1969 by the Connecticut Historical Commission for development as
a museum of Black history, culture, and achievement.

Miss Crandall's school for young ladies opened its doors in November, 1831, in propitious circumstances. Canterbury was happy; so was Prudence. No doubt so were Pardon and Esther, to have their daughter so close. Eighteen-year-old Almira, described later by William Lloyd Garrison as "a beautiful girl," was pleased by her big sister's enterprise, for she was to have a part in it.

Not only did the girls of Canterbury have their school right there, but other young ladies from quite distant towns made application and were admitted as boarders. A year later, something happened which Prudence herself summed up, a long time afterwards, in a letter:

"I had a nice colored girl, now Mrs. Charles Harris, as help in my family; and her intended husband regularly received *The Liberator* [William Lloyd Garrison's radical Abolitionist newspaper, published in Boston]. The girl took the paper from the office and loaned it to me. In that the condition of the colored people both slaves and free was truthfully portrayed . . . and the question of Immediate Emancipation of the millions of slaves in the United States boldly advocated. Having been taught from early childhood the sin of Slavery, my sympathies were greatly aroused. Sarah Harris, a respectable young woman and a member of the church (now Mrs. Fairweather, and sister to the before-named intended husband), called often to see her friend Marcia, my family assistant. In some of her calls I ascertained that she wished to attend my school and board at her own father's house at some little distance from the village. I allowed her to enter as one of my pupils. By this act I gave great offense. . . . I very soon found that some of my school would leave not to return if the colored girl was retained."

The town was greatly upset, thought it ungrateful and very bad form of Miss Crandall to behave so, but felt reasonably sure that she would come to her senses when faced by the threatened withdrawals. But the spark ignited by *The Libera-*

tor was burning in Prudence's mind. In mid-January, 1833, she wrote to William Lloyd Garrison, and late in the month turned up in Boston to see him personally. Then she went back to Canterbury, but a few days later took the boat from Providence to New York and had some conversations there, with persons suggested by Garrison.

Canterbury suspected nothing; tranquillity lay over the Green. The bomb burst publicly in *The Liberator*, March 2, 1833, in a small advertisement inserted by Prudence, announcing the opening in Canterbury of "a High School for young colored Ladies and Misses." The families of the white pupils, who did not read *The Liberator*, had got the shock about a week earlier through their own daughters, sent home to report that since the white school of Canterbury could not receive colored girls, it would thereafter cater specifically to colored girls. It was not that Prudence would reject a white girl—but after that, who would send one?

The battle was joined, but in the consternation and confusion of this first stage, the patterns it would take could not be foreseen. The outraged people of the town did not yet know just what they would do, but they would do something.

The genteel Quaker lady showed herself hooped with steel. She did not quail before the indignant parties that called upon her to express their outrage. With one such delegation, Esquire Frost, in what was reported by the village side as "a most kind and affecting manner," pointed out to her, delicately, that these "leveling principles" might result in "intermarriage between the whites and blacks." Prudence gave him a cold eye and snapped, "Moses had a black wife!"

[CHAPTER III]

Of Purity of
Motives

THE WAY THE HAPPY PROGRESS OF THE CANTERBURY SCHOOL
was impeded, as it began its second year in 1832, depends
partly on whose version you are reading. We have seen already,
in the letter written by Prudence a long time afterwards, that
she admitted the Negro girl, Sarah Harris, as a pupil, and
apparently was taken by surprise at the objections raised.

Closer to the event, in a statement published in *The Liberator*, May 25, 1833, we see that she was not so simple as to
think the move would bring no reaction:

"A colored girl of respectability—a professor of religion
—and daughter of respectable parents called on me some time
during the month of September last, and said in a very earnest
manner, 'Miss Crandall, I want to get a little more learning,
enough if possible to teach colored children, and if you will admit me to your school, I shall forever be under the greatest obligation to you. If you think it will be the means of injuring
you, I will not insist on the favor.'

"I did not answer her immediately, as I thought perhaps,
if I gave her permission some of my scholars might be disturbed. In further conversation with her, however, I found she
had a great anxiety to improve in learning.

"Her repeated solicitations were more than my feelings
could resist, and I told her if I was injured on her account I
would bear it—she might enter as one of my pupils."

Sarah was of light complexion. In the district public school, at a younger age, she had attended classes with some of the same town girls among whom her presence was thought unacceptable now. She was acknowledged as a member of the congregation in the church. As in some later cases, down to the present time, it was not Sarah's fellow pupils who made the objections, but their parents. As May put it, "Sarah belonged to the proscribed, despised class, and therefore must not be admitted into a private school with their daughters."

Sarah Harris worked in the house of Jedediah Shephard, where another Negro girl, Mary Barber, also was employed. Mary, in written testimony solicited from her by Prudence's opposition gave a slightly varying account which was introduced at the trial. According to Mary, Prudence first asked Sarah about the extent of her education, and upon hearing it was poor, invited her to come to school, where, in a year or so, she could be prepared for teaching. Mary claimed that Sarah said "that she should never have thought of going if Miss Crandall had not *proposed* it to her, and she had concluded to go."

Objections to Sarah's presence were quick to come, from several persons. In one instance, as Prudence related it: "The wife of an Episcopal clergyman who lived in the village [though there was no Episcopal church there] told me that if I continued that colored girl in my school, it could not be sustained. I replied to her *That it might sink, then, for I should not turn her out!*"

Probably the townspeople believed that Prudence could be made to listen to persuasion. She, on the other hand, evidently wasted no time wondering whether her neighbors might be persuaded to accept Sarah Harris's presence. In January and February, 1833, she wrote three letters to the country's most notorious radical Abolitionist, William Lloyd Garrison, whose journal *The Liberator,* as we have seen, had blown into flame the spark of concern about the colored people which Prudence already carried because of her Quaker education.

Here is the first of those letters:

Canterbury, Jan. 18th, 1833.

Mr. Garrison: I am to you, sir, I presume, an entire stranger, and you are indeed so to me save through the medium of the public print. I am by no means fond of egotism, but the circumstances under which I labor forbid my asking a friend to write for me; therefore I will tell you who I am, and for what purpose I write. I am, sir, through the blessing of divine Providence, permitted to be the Principal of the Canterbury (Conn.) Female Boarding School. I received a considerable part of my education at the Friends' Boarding School, Providence, R. I. In 1831 I purchased a large dwelling-house in the centre of this village, and opened the school above mentioned. Since I commenced I have met with all the encouragement I ever anticipated, and now have a flourishing school.

Now I will tell you why I write you, and the object is this: I wish to know your opinion respecting changing white scholars for colored ones. I have been for some months past determined if possible during the remaining part of my life to benefit the people of color. I do not dare tell any one of my neighbors anything about the contemplated change in my school, and I beg of you, sir, that you will not expose it to any one; for if it was known, I have no reason to expect but it would ruin my present school. Will you be so kind as to write by the next mail and give me your opinion on the subject; and if you consider it possible to obtain 20 or 25 young ladies of color to enter this school for the term of one year at the rate of $25 per quarter, including board, washing, and tuition, I will come to Boston in a few days and make some arrangements about it. I do not suppose that number can be obtained in Boston alone; but from all the large cities in the several States I thought perhaps they might be gathered.

I must once more beg you not to expose this matter until we see how the case will be determined.

Yours, with the greatest respect,

Prudence Crandall.

On the twenty-ninth, she was in Boston and sent a note requesting Garrison to call upon her at six in the evening, at the Marlboro Hotel on Washington Street. This was the station for the Providence stage, by which she had arrived. Garrison met her there, encouraged her in the project, and suggested people that she might see, for various forms of aid, in both Providence and New York.

On the way home, Prudence stopped in Providence. There she visited, at Garrison's suggestion, a Mrs. Hammond, whose seventeen-year-old daughter Ann Eliza would become one of the pupils in the reconstituted school. Mrs. Hammond also introduced her to two young white men George W. and Henry E. Benson, who were interested in the cause. They were sons of the elder George W. Benson, Samuel May's retired friend in Brooklyn, and brothers of that Mary, not yet known to her, who would later share her jail cell for a night in Brooklyn. Henry Benson wrote Garrison: "The lady who was at your office last week to see about a school for colored females, passed through here Friday. . . . She is, I should think, exactly the one for that purpose, and I hope she may meet with perfect success."

Mrs. Hammond also walked about with Prudence to the homes of several other Negro families, with the result that six girls, at a minimum, seemed likely prospects from Providence.

Back in Canterbury, Prudence now first confided her scheme to a local man, clearly under a promise that he would keep his counsel. That was one of her board of visitors, Captain Daniel Packer, a manufacturer. He lived in a hamlet called Packerville, two or three miles to the south, and was the founder of the Baptist church there.

Evidently Prudence knew the temper of his conscience. But Packer was disturbed, as she wrote to Garrison: "He said he thought the object to be praiseworthy, but he was very much troubled about the result . . . he thinks I shall injure myself in the undertaking."

A few days later she was off to New York, via boat, a twice-weekly service which once gave rise to a punning exchange in New York: "I'm off to Boston." "How are you going?" *"Deo volente."* "Which way is that?" "By way of Providence." A local friend, most likely Sarah Harris's brother Charles, an agent for *The Liberator* through whom Prudence had begun to read that paper, gave her an introduction to a Negro minister in New York. Garrison had given her the names of several of his friends, most notably the wealthy merchant and Abolitionist Arthur Tappan, and promised that he would write to them about her. Other than those links, she had "not the least acquaintance there." As she told Garrison, "When I return from N. Y., I think I shall be able to lay the subject before the public." After the trip, she had initial prospects of at least twenty colored girls from New York, Philadelphia, Boston, and Providence.

Those journeys to Boston, Providence, and New York became the focus of bitter charges of bad faith and stealth against Prudence. Richard Fenner, a storekeeper, a supporter of the original school, and one of the committee that called to remonstrate with Prudence after her plan was made known, made a formal deposition for use in the second trial. He alleged that she "came into my store, and without any knowledge on my part that she was going to Boston, and without any request from me, or anyone else, she voluntarily told me that she was going to Boston to visit the infant schools and purchase an infant school apparatus, and asked me for a letter of introduction to some of my friends there. She made no mention of any other business she had there, except what is above stated, and this she did in such a manner as to preclude any belief that she had any other business."

There is no indication that Prudence did anything at all in connection with such alleged intentions about an infants school. It seems to have been a smoke screen. She had further said that the purchasing of equipment was the reason for the New York trip. In a letter during the height of the controversy she said that her failure to buy equipment on those trips was due to lack of funds. Her opponents wondered out loud why she went to buy equipment if she knew she had not the money to pay for it.

Purity of motives is always a complex question. There is no doubt that Prudence believed deeply in her cause, and that her commitment of conscience to it increased steadily from the birth of the idea and her earliest moves to carry it out. But there is also no doubt that Prudence was a difficult person. It is fair to say that she did dissemble, and that she acted with remarkable precipitateness and secrecy considering the aid and support that her townsmen had given her in the original school, for which she had often expressed gratitude. Obstinacy and anger appear to be involved in the abruptness and drastic extreme of her response to the town's resistance to the admission of a colored girl. She could have pursued principle with greater candor, even with no less determination. As it was, she appears to have determined, perhaps unconsciously, to let them have it with both barrels, which is exactly what she did—even if it were in a righteous cause. In her old age, Prudence told a visiting journalist in Kansas, "My whole life has been one of opposition." We must not lose sight of that truth about Prudence's temperament, even while recognizing the genuineness of her convictions and history's endorsement of her actions.

CHAPTER IV

The Blowup

THE FURY OF THE TOWN AROSE FROM A MIXTURE OF SHOCK at the idea of a colored school in their midst and of understandable resentment of the way Prudence had gone about her plan. Their daughters arrived home one day, around February 20, 1833, bringing the news that they were not to go back, that they were dismissed to make room for black boarding students from far places. Only later did they learn of the advertisement for the school, in *The Liberator,* which began to run on March 2 and continued in the paper until the school was disbanded. There could not be a more extreme case of calculatedly bad public relations.

It was the next day that Messrs. Adams, Frost, Harris, and Fenner, sounding much like a brokerage house or law partnership, waited on her to try to dissuade her from the scheme. They expressed only kindly feelings toward the colored race. What she wished to do, they said in effect, was a good thing to do—*elsewhere.* There were pitfalls in such a plan. That was when Frost, hinting "in a kind and affecting manner" of the dangers of racial intermarriage, got the crisp rebuff, "Moses had a black wife." It was clear that no compromise or conciliation whatsoever was to be expected from the Quaker lady. It was a standoff. The callers withdrew. Work went on in the house on the Green, to prepare to receive the influx of boarding students on the announced opening date, April 1.

Since private persuasion did not work, public action was

The Prudence Crandall house, Canterbury, Connecticut. Photo by Charles Spurgeon, 1970.

Arnold Buffum

ARNOLD BUFFUM. Engraved from a portrait, ca. 1824. Reproduced from *William Lloyd Garrison, 1805-1879: The Story of His Life Told by His Children.*

tried. A town meeting was called for the ninth of March, in the Congregational church, to consider the problem "townwise," as a contemporary report put it. The words of the "warning," or notice, described the meeting as called "to devise and adopt such measures as would effectually avert the nuisance, or speedily abate it if it should be brought into the village."

The central figure of the controversy need only have walked across the road to attend, but deemed it prudent not to appear in person. For her to do so, or to speak in public in her own behalf, was held to be unseemly and unwomanly in the mores of the time and place.

The Reverend Samuel J. May, in Brooklyn, six miles to the north, had heard about the Canterbury affair. He decided that he must make some move about it, though he did so in the awareness that he might further inflame matters. So he wrote to Prudence, on February 28, saying that upon hearing of her plans and the resistance to them, "although I am a stranger to you," he felt "determined to do all in my power to assist you."

One possible handicap was that he was a Unitarian minister in a stronghold of Calvinistic Congregationalism which had a turbulent history of theological quarrels. May knew that even Prudence, as a Quaker, might disapprove of his doctrines. He spoke of all this, candidly:

"You are probably well aware that my religious sentiments have rendered me obnoxious to the suspicion and ill-will of the Clergy, and a considerable proportion of the people in this vicinity. This may lessen very much my ability to serve you. But I wish you would command my services in any way in which you think I can be useful to you. . . ."

Even in that first letter he made a suggestion that would be pressed further:

"It has occurred to me that your *conspicuous* residence in the village might render your plan more objectionable to those, who are so hostile to the blacks. Perhaps your removal

to some more retired situation would at once allay the violence of your opponents, and be more favorable to your pupils,
who would not be so exposed to insult as they might be where
you now are.

"I should be very happy to see you at my house—or I
will come and see you, if a visit, from such a heretic as I am
accounted, would not increase the ill-will of your neighbors
toward you. . . ."

Prudence replied promptly to "Friend May," asking him
to visit her as soon as he could. At once, on the fourth of
March, May drove down to Canterbury, taking along his
friend George W. Benson. As they were seen entering the town,
someone—May does not make it clear whether it was a friend
or an enemy—warned him that if he showed himself as Prudence's friend he would bring the wrath of the town against
him. The mood of the town had become disorderly. Insults
were hurled at Prudence and anyone showing any sympathy
for her.

May found her "resolved and tranquil. The effect of her
Quaker discipline appeared in every word she spoke, and in
every expression of her countenance." As she could find no
advocate in town for the pending meeting, she begged, "Will
not you, Friend May, be my attorney?" He pledged himself
to do so, and after some discussion of tactics, went home.

On her part, Prudence missed no chance to procure further counsel. She learned that Arnold Buffum, a fellow Quaker
and the principal lecturing agent of the New-England Anti-
Slavery Society, was in Norwich. On March 8, the day before
the town meeting, she went there and persuaded him to come
to Canterbury to support her case. It was with surprise, but
pleasure, that May found Buffum also on hand when he arrived in Canterbury on the day of the meeting.

Buffum, then fifty-one, with at least five generations behind him on American soil, had grown up in Rhode Island,
where his father, both farmer and merchant, ran an active sta-

tion of the Underground Railroad. Contact with many fugitives passing through his house drew the young man into dedicated concern for the abolition of slavery.

Buffum had little formal education. He became a hatter and in the Yankee mechanical tradition invented several devices useful to the hatmaking trade. Just about a year before the present crisis in Canterbury, he had been a founder of the New-England Anti-Slavery Society, and became its first president as well as its chief spokesman. By now this cause had drawn him almost wholly from his trade. He was an eloquent speaker and writer, a reminder that the phrase "little formal education" did not mean then what it means now. Elementary schooling, in those days, carried a man further in articulateness and clarity of argument than college does for many today.

Both Benson brothers had come from Providence, Henry officially to report the meeting for *The Liberator*. Garrison was sharply attentive to what was afoot in Canterbury. He had written to Benson:

"If possible, Miss Crandall must be sustained at all hazards. If we suffer the school to be put down in Canterbury, other places will partake of the panic, and also prevent its introduction in their vicinity. We may as well, 'first as last,' meet this proscriptive spirit, *and conquer it*. We—i. e., all true friends of the cause—must make this a common concern. The New Haven excitement has furnished a bad precedent; a second must not be given, or I know not what we can do to raise up the colored population in a manner which their intellectual and moral necessities demand. In Boston we are all excited at the Canterbury affair."

In the reference to New Haven there are intimations, which we shall pursue shortly, of broader ramifications to the problems of blacks and whites in Connecticut.

Now May and Buffum reviewed with the beleaguered schoolmistress the strategy for the meeting across the road. As outsiders, a point of which much would be made, they had no right to be heard on their own account in this town meeting. Prudence gave to each of them a separate letter to the moderator, requesting formally that each man, in turn, might be heard on her behalf. It was stipulated that Buffum was her primary spokesman, May the secondary one, but that each had points to make. The letters also affirmed that they were authorized to negotiate a compromise with the community on her behalf and that she would abide by any agreement they might reach.

When the two men walked across the road, the meeting-house was already jammed. John C. Kimball, one of the earliest chroniclers of the affair (1886), used mock-heroic prose to describe the town hall "crammed from floor to gallery with Canterbury's alarmed free men, the sons of sires who had been with Putnam when of old he had dragged the wolf from her den, and had stood shoulder to shoulder with each other in many a bloody fight against England's invading hosts, rushing now from shop, store and field to drag this more insidious Quaker wolf from her den and to repel these more formidable 'misses of color' from their soil."

Meanwhile, the Benson brothers—young men of staid bearing who were somewhat ludicrously denounced, later, as "boisterous boys," when Henry (actually nineteen) was observed to be making notes—had managed to get into the crowded gallery, which in the architectural tradition of New England Congregationalism was U-shaped, extending along the sides almost the whole length of the building. The advocates squeezed their way down a side aisle "into the wall-pew next to the deacon's seat, in which sat the Moderator," who was Asael Bacon, Esq. Their presence called forth scowls and offensive comments from people around them. Concentrated xenophobia was moving toward alarming absurdity. A few local colored men were also in the balcony. They remained quiet throughout and no particular hostility was manifested toward them. There was no more worried spectator in the throng than Pardon Crandall, watching his neighbors' wrath against his eldest daughter.

When the meeting was called to order and the "warning" or notice of its purpose had been duly read, Rufus Adams, Justice of the Peace, introduced the following resolutions:

WHEREAS, it hath been publicly announced that a school is to be opened in this town, on the first Monday of April next, using the language of the advertisement, "for young ladies and little misses of color," or in other words for the people of color, the obvious tendency of which would be to collect within the town of Canterbury large numbers of persons from other States whose characters and habits might be various and unknown to us, thereby rendering insecure the persons, property and reputations of our citizens. Under such circumstances our silence might be construed into an approbation of the project;

Thereupon, Resolved, That the locality of a school for the people of color at any place within the limits of this town, for the admission of persons of foreign jurisdiction, meets with our unqualified disapprobation, and it is to be understood, that the inhabitants of Canterbury protest against it in the most earnest manner.

Resolved, That a committee be now appointed, to be composed of the Civil Authority and Selectmen, who shall make known to the person contemplating the establishment of said school, the sentiments and objections entertained by this meeting in reference to said school—pointing out to her the injurious effects and incalculable evils resulting from such an establishment within this town, and persuade her to abandon the project.

Judge Adams, as the town called him, glossed the reading of the resolutions with sharp criticism of Prudence and questioning of her motives.

The next speaker was her neighbor Andrew T. Judson.

There is no doubt, as May wrote later, that he was, throughout, "chief of Miss Crandall's persecutors. He was the great man of the town, a leading politician in the State much talked of by the Democrats as soon to be governor, and a few years afterwards was appointed Judge of the United States District Court."

Judson and May had been respectful acquaintances, almost friends. In an open letter to Judson, some three weeks after the meeting, May gave his own description of the great man's speech. "You twanged every chord that could stir the coarser passions of the human heart; and with such sad success that your hearers seemed to have lost for the time their perception of right and wrong." Judson talked of "calamity" pending the town, declining property values, subverted morals, mongrelization, threatened by "this nigger school." Miss Crandall he depicted as the tool of "powerful conspirators," of "foreign interference" by people from abroad —"abroad" meaning as little as six miles away. He hinted at great wealth and influence behind the plot.

Judson had churned up the meeting. Buffum and May felt it was Prudence's turn. First Buffum, then May, leaned across the pew and handed their letters to Moderator Bacon. He read them and handed them on to Judson, who glanced at them, then angrily denounced the two outsiders for an insulting meddlesomeness in Canterbury's affairs. Other angry cries backed him up. The moderator ruled that they could not address the meeting, and warned that if they tried to do so they would be prosecuted. Buffum and May, neither of whom had said anything, kept silent. The chief spokesmen for the town had been heard, the resolutions had been passed. The meeting was adjourned.

The moment after adjournment, May stood up on his pew and cried out, in style reminiscent of St. Paul on Mars hill in Athens: "Men of Canterbury, I have a word for you! Hear me!" Curiosity warring with hostility, a good many stopped their progress to the doors and listened. He launched into a brief defense of Prudence and rebuttal of what he called the misrepresentations of her character and her plan. Then he yielded to Buffum, who stated Prudence's willingness to sell her house for what it had cost her and establish her school in some more remote part of the village. One guesses that she may have had her parents' farm in mind.

A certain George S. White, the only moderate voice heard that night among the townspeople, offered to contribute to the purchase of the house from Prudence. But the opposition, caught off guard by this post-adjournment tactic, had regrouped. Trustees of the church now re-entered and demanded that Buffum and May leave the building at once, that the doors might be locked. They were backed by cries of "Out, out, out!"

Again Prudence's supporters obeyed scrupulously. They left the church but stood for some time on the Green, answering questions and seeking to persuade any who would listen to them. When this rump meeting broke up, May and Buffum departed, the Unitarian recording afterwards that he felt, like the Apostles at Ephesus, "in danger to be called in question for this day's uproar."

Of this, even a pamphlet hostile to Prudence, called "Statement of Facts," issued by a Brooklyn, Connecticut, press, conceded in a footnote: "There was *one* step taken, which cannot be accounted for in any other way than by charging it to the exciting circumstances of the occasion . . . refusing to listen, after the town meeting had been dissolved, to those whom Miss Crandall had engaged to speak for her. . . . After the meeting had been broken up, a proper sense of justice would seem to secure for them the privilege of speaking to the people, if they were disposed to hear. Those who had charge of the meetinghouse, it will be remembered, directed the gentlemen to retire, that the house might be closed."

CHAPTER V

Bells and Cannon

THE BOASTFULLY IRRESISTIBLE FORCE OF PREJUDICE HAD MET the proudly immovable object of righteousness.

Andrew T. Judson was both lawyer and politician. In the wake of the turbulent town meeting where he had been the prime swayer of passions, he seems to have had second thoughts. May had enjoyed what he called "a pleasant acquaintance" with Judson. The lawyer now sought to mend fences somewhat.

Two days after the meeting he called on May, in Brooklyn, expressing regret at his own possible extremism in the heat of argument. There had been no personal rancor, he wished to assure him, though he still felt that May was "inconsiderately and unjustly promoting" the Crandall scheme.

May then said that if Buffum and he had been allowed to speak to the formal meeting, they would have made an offer to negotiate for the sale of the Crandall house and the moving of the school to some remote quarter of the town. Judson's response to this, as reported by May, for the first time drew the lines unequivocally:

"Mr. May, we are not merely opposed to the establishment of that school in Canterbury; we mean there shall not be such a school set up anywhere in our State. The colored people can never rise from their menial condition in our country; they ought not to be permitted to rise here. They are an inferior race of beings, and never can or ought to be recognized as the equals of the whites. Africa is the place for them. I am in favor of the Colonization scheme. Let the niggers and their descendants be sent back to their fatherland; and there improve themselves as much as they may, and civilize and Christianize the natives, if they can. I am a Colonizationist. You and your friend Garrison have undertaken what you cannot accomplish. The condition of the colored population of our country can never be essentially improved on this continent. You are fanatical about them. You are violating the Constitution of our Republic, which settled forever the status of the black men in this land. They belong to Africa. Let them be sent back there, or kept as they are here. The sooner you Abolitionists abandon your project the better for our country, for the niggers, and yourselves."

May replied: "Mr. Judson, there never will be fewer colored people in this country than there are now. Of the vast majority of them this is the native land, as much as it is ours. . . . The only question is, whether we will recognize the rights which God gave them as men, and encourage and assist them to become all he has made them capable of being, or whether we will continue wickedly to deny them the privileges we enjoy, condemn them to degradation, enslave and imbrute them; and so bring upon ourselves the condemnation of the Almighty Impartial Father of all men, and the terrible visitation of the God of the oppressed. . . . If you and your neighbors in Canterbury had quietly consented that Sarah Harris, whom you knew to be a bright, good girl, should enjoy the privilege she so eagerly sought, this momentous conflict would not have arisen in your village. But as it has arisen there, we may as well meet it there as elsewhere."

Judson reiterated angrily: "No—that school shall not be located in any part of the town of Canterbury; no—not in any part of the State of Connecticut. I will get a law passed by our next Legislature, prohibiting the introduction of colored children from other States into this for the purpose of attending school. I can obtain thirty thousand signers to a petition for such a Law."

May said he would fight such an attempt in the Legislature and in the courts.

Judson cried: "You talk big; it will cost more than you are aware of to do all that you threaten. Where will you get the means to carry on such a contest at law?"

May confessed he could not answer that except by faith. Then, "Mr. Judson left me in high displeasure, and I never met him afterwards but as an opponent."

On the fourteenth of March, five days after the town meeting, a committee of the Selectmen and other citizens called upon Miss Crandall, pursuant to the resolutions, to urge her once more to desist from her plans. This time they offered to purchase back her house, but she must not merely move the site of her school; she must abandon the project. She refused.

April first came and with it that visitation which the town had dreaded as if it were one of the plagues of Egypt. Some fifteen to twenty well-bred colored girls arrived at the school. They came from Providence, Boston, New York, and Philadelphia, and in their ranks, of course, was Canterbury's Sarah Harris whose case had precipitated the whole enterprise. The precise number of students is not clear nor is it certain exactly how they were lodged. Apparently most and perhaps all of them were in the schoolhouse itself, though conceivably some may have lodged at Pardon Crandall's farmhouse. Prudence's younger sister Almira had thrown herself into the cause and aided in teaching and all the other operations of the school. She is often named, with Prudence, as a defendant in the subsequent legal actions.

The townspeople met and issued yet another resolution, its prose style indicating the pitch to which they had wrought themselves, asserting that "the establishment, or rendezvous, planted in their midst, falsely denominated a school, was designed by its projectors as the theatre in which to promulgate their disgusting doctrines of amalgamation, and their pernicious sentiments subverting the Union, and to educate pupils to scatter fire-brands, arrows and death among brethren of our own blood."

Boycotts were applied to almost every need of the school. Though Canterbury was an important stage-route crossing, the stage drivers, mindful of the patronage of the influential citizens, refused to carry any of the pupils. Frederick Olney; a colored man from Norwich, with a wagon, transported the girls, and sometimes in the ensuing months performed the same service for some of the visiting Abolitionists.

None of the local stores would sell Prudence any merchandise. For all her needs she had to rely on distant communities, and all supplies, including food of course—even the milk-peddler refused her—had to be brought from a distance by her father or some one of her tiny band of friends. The local physicians, following the lead of Dr. Harris, refused to give medical services—Hippocratic oath be damned!

All the pupils, like their teacher, were pious Christians, but the church doors were closed to them in Canterbury, though before the crisis the town's few Negroes had worshipped there regularly. The Reverend Levi Kneeland of the Baptist church at Packerville welcomed them, as did a Quaker meeting at outlying Black Hill, but these places were hard to reach, the means of travel were not available, and every venture out of doors for the school was a form of skirmish. So the Reverends Kneeland, May, and other occasional visiting clergy sometimes held worship services at the school.

When pupils and teachers went for exercise walks, stones, sticks, rotten eggs, pellets of manure, dead cats, chicken heads, and other repulsive missiles frequently were flung at them, chiefly by boys with the complaisant tolerance of their parents. The opponents claimed, in print, that "Whenever any thing of the kind was resorted to, it was the work of boyish folly, or is chargeable upon some of the blacks belonging to the neighborhood."

Manure was smeared over the school's doors and doorsteps, and to more serious effect was dumped in the well. Thereafter they were dependent for water upon the distressed and frightened Pardon Crandall, who brought what he could from his farm under constant threat and abuse.

Garrison, on a visit to Canterbury to observe the school in action (a side excursion from his courtship visits to the Benson home, but still a matter of high concern) reported that the school was "in the full tide of successful experiment." But he noted also "the stone which was thrown into the window by some unknown republican of Canterbury—the shattered pane of glass—the window-curtain stained by a volley of rotten eggs—and last, not least, a moral nondescript, though physically a human being, named A—— T—— J——."

Garrison's presence in town was no secret, indeed was flaunted. On previous visits, the sheriff had pursued him to the Bensons' home in Brooklyn, trying to serve him with five summonses in complaint for libel, from Judson and other Canterburians angered by Garrison's invective against them in *The Liberator*. This time the sheriff found him, near midnight, at the Bensons, and served the papers. Though several dates were set and changed, the libel case never came to trial, the plaintiffs evidently reconsidering lest they stir up more hornets.

The town officers attempted to invoke an obsolete vagrancy law, in keeping with their professed anxiety that this flood of alien black girls was likely to leave a residue of paupers stranded at the expense of the town. Any individual warned by the selectmen to get out of town under the vagrancy act became subject to a series of fines up to a time of ten days, after which the offender, male or female, if still in town, was to be "whipped on the naked body not exceeding ten stripes."

A warrant was served under the law upon Ann Eliza Hammond a seventeen-year-old student from Providence. Samuel May went into action at once. He knew it was a bluff, intended to frighten the girls besieged far from home in a wilderness of white antipathy and latent violence. He deposited with the town treasurer of Canterbury a bond in the amount of $10,000, put up by the elder Benson, as a guarantee against the vagrancy of any pupil and resultant cost to the town.

Also he talked with the girls, telling Ann Eliza that he was certain the town officials would not dare proceed to the extremity of the public whipping, "knowing that every blow they should strike her would resound throughout the land, if not over the civilized world, and call out an expression of indignation before which Mr. Judson and his associates would quail." He found the girl calm and willing to accept that remote possibility of whipping for the sake of the support it would rally to their cause.

Judson and company, meanwhile, had been busy in Hartford with the legislature. They filed petitions for aid against Prudence. The case was assigned to a committee, which in May submitted a report and a bill for consideration of the lawmakers.

The language of the report, signed by the committee chairman, Philip Pearl, Jr., is striking in its ambivalence. It condemns slavery in terms worthy of Garrison. It notes with pride:

> It is about half a century since the Legislature of this State commenced a system for gradual abolition of slavery, and the great object has been consummated, still the unhappy class of beings, whose race has been degraded by unjust bondage, are among us, and justly demand at our hands all which

is consistent with the common safety, and their own best interest, for the amelioration of their state and character.

Of Connecticut the document further observes:

Our whole population of color, born within the last century, are already restored to the blessings of freedom.* The constitution and laws of the State have secured to them all the rights and privileges of other citizens, except that of the elective franchise, and those to which it is essential.

But the report moved rapidly toward its aim:

In regard to the education of all those of that unfortunate class of beings who belong to this State, the Legislature ought not to impede, but so far as may be within their province, and consistent with the best interest of the people, to foster and sustain the benevolent efforts of individuals directed to that end. Here our *duties* terminate. The colored people of *other States,* and *other countries,* are under the laws and guardianship of their respective sovereignties, and *we* are not entrusted with the powers of enquiring into the expediency or justice of their local regulations, except to acquire wisdom in regard to *our own.* Here are the boundaries of our Legislative rights and *duties.* We are under no obligation, moral or political, to incur the incalculable evils, of bringing into *our own State,* colored emigrants from abroad. For this we have the example of other members of our confederacy by whom slavery is tolerated. It is a fact confirmed by painful and long experience, and one that results from the condition of the colored people, in the midst of a white population, in all States and countries, that they are an appalling source of crime and pauperism. As this, in our own State, proceeds from the degradation to which their

* This claim was not completely true. The number of slaves in Connecticut had diminished greatly since the beginning of the century, but at the time of these events there were some twenty slaves in the state and some were to be found there as late as 1848.

ancestors have been wrongfully subjected, it imposes on us an imperious duty, to advance their morals and usefulness, and preserve them so far as possible from the evils which they have been obliged to inherit, but at the same time the duty is not less imperative, to protect *our own citizens,* against that host of colored emigrants, which would rush in from every quarter, when invited to our colleges and schools. . . .

Although the introduction of colored persons for the purposes of education merely, would seem to contemplate but a temporary residence, yet that class of people have seldom any settled establishments in their own States, or other inducements to return, after the period of instruction has expired; and as their last association and attachments would be here;—a great portion of the whole number would make this State their permanent residence. The immense evils which such a mass of colored population, as would gather within this State, when it has become their place of resort from *other States* and from other countries, would impose on our own people burthens which would admit of no future remedy and can be avoided only by timely prevention.

Conceding that "Particular instances may occur in which the admission of a colored person belonging to any other State, to the privileges of a school, might be justified from peculiar circumstances," the report continues its blend of pious generalization with cautious protectionism by saying that in each town "It would seem both safe and just to place the subject under the direction of their own *civil authority and selectmen.*"

This report was offered to the Legislature together with a bill bearing the curiously complicated heading: "An Act in addition to an Act entitled 'An Act for the admission and settlement of Inhabitants in Towns.'" The vital provision of the bill was:

Be it enacted by the Senate and House of Representatives, in General Assembly convened, That no person shall set up or establish in this State any school, academy, or literary institution, for the instruction or education of colored persons who are not inhabitants of this State, nor instruct or teach in any school, academy, or literary institution whatsoever in this State, or harbor or board, for the purpose of attending or being taught or instructed in any such school, academy or literary institution, any colored person who is not an inhabitant of any town in this State, without the consent, in writing, first obtained of a majority of the civil authority, and also of the select-men of the town in which such school, academy, or literary institution is situated; and each and every person who shall knowingly do an act forbidden as aforesaid, or shall be aiding or assisting therein; shall, for the first offence, forfeit and pay to the treasurer of this State, a fine of one hundred dollars, and for the second offence shall forfeit and pay a fine of two hundred dollars, and so double for every offence of which he or she shall be convicted. . . .

That bill, which became notorious as Connecticut's "Black Law," was passed by Senate and House of Representatives and approved by the Governor, May 24, 1833. If there were any opposition in debate, or any nay votes cast, which is probable, the accounts do not say. The prevailing sentiment of the legislators, and by inference of their constituents, was clear. It was upon charges under that law, written specifically to put an end to her school, that Prudence Crandall was arrested on June 27 and jailed that same day—the episode with which this book opened.

Samuel May reported: "On receipt of the tidings that the Legislature had passed the law, joy and exultation ran wild in Canterbury. The bells were rung and a cannon fired, until all the inhabitants for miles around were informed of the triumph."

CHAPTER VI

Canterbury

Now we have a change of pace and a shift of focus in the Canterbury tale. In a sense it ceases to be Prudence Crandall's personal story, or is less so, from the time of the town meeting at which Buffum and May tried to speak for her. Behind everything still remains the rock of Prudence's will, her fixity of purpose. But her personal energies were expended chiefly within the walls of her school. In keeping with the mores of the age, and as a practical matter of legal battles, others, males, "outsiders," had the management of the case. Prudence is more a presence than an actor at her trials. True, she gave testimony at the first one, but the substance of that testimony was never in dispute. It is the constitutional issues that are the drama behind the seeming legalistic dryness of the trials and appeal.

Since now it is a struggle of the town against the professionals, since national constitutional issues are at stake, we should step aside for a while from Prudence and look closely at this town of Canterbury and the traditions and precedents in its history that prepared the ground for this clash. Then we must consider those skilled zealots, the Abolitionists, who took over the management of Prudence's case. Then we shall examine some of the larger contexts, in both the State of Connecticut and the nation at large, in the perspective of which the Canterbury case should be seen.

Driving from Providence to Canterbury today, one may follow Route 6 west to Brooklyn, Connecticut. That is not the fastest way, but it takes one through the Reverend Samuel J. May's town and on to Canterbury via a road much travelled by the principals during the agitation.

Approaching Brooklyn, one is struck by scenes that Samuel May could not have encountered even in his nightmares: the highway garishness of Dairy Kremes and Pizzaramas. But the village itself is still quite small. At its heart, and off Route 6, the beautiful old houses still stand, there is a sense of quiet, and many of the great elms and maples Samuel May loved still line the streets. The road south to Canterbury, once boasting the important name of Worcester-Norwich turnpike, now Connecticut 169, is paved and in reasonably good shape but is no longer even a secondary road. It would be hard to rank—tertiary, quaternary?

But the six miles between the towns are still beautiful and tranquil. The way is not heavily built up. Samuel May could drive it with some recognition. The gentle, rolling valley, with distant hills to the east, is farm country. One passes the Israel Putnam State monument, commemorating Brooklyn's Revolutionary War hero, and a few houses. Then there is Canterbury. If, like this traveller, one arrived hungry, planning to lunch there, he would find it impossible to do so except by buying something from the grocer's shelves.

Canterbury has diminished. It has less people, less influence, less importance than in Prudence's day. It is a crossroad at which are clustered a few old houses, a food market, and a filling station. Prudence's house cannot be missed. It is occupied, well kept up—a vintage piece of early New England architecture. A sign on a post by the fence proclaims that Prudence Crandall once kept a school for colored girls there. Regrettably, it gives no hint of the troubles.

A few other houses, some well kept up, others declining, still stand. The Congregational church is there, the chief difference in appearance from older days being a small, gravelled parking lot beside it. There was no resident minister in the summer of 1968, when one was sought in the hope that he might know the lore of the town. Behind the church was a small, paint-faded frame building with a sign "Canterbury Library." It was padlocked and looked unused.

What has preserved the rural quiet of Canterbury, but also accounts for its diminishment, is the fact that the Connecticut Turnpike sweeps the modern traffic flow past Plainfield, about four miles east. Canterbury has never had a major function in the age of the automobile, except as a place to escape from it.

Canterbury is in the valley of the Quinebaug River, in Windham County. The original Windham town line followed what was called the Nipmuck Path, defined by Uncas, the Mohican glorified by Fenimore Cooper but considered by the Puritans "an old and wicked, wilful man, a drunkard, and otherwise very vicious; who has always been an opposer and underminer of praying to God." The region was highly important in the expansion of the colonies and the development of Connecticut. It suffered in the Pequot Indian wars.

Plainfield was established as a town in 1700. In 1703, a hundred years before Prudence was born, Canterbury came into separate existence, with that old Nipmuck Path a part of its boundaries with Plainfield. The separation of the towns came about because of the Quinebaug, which flows between them. It is one of several tributaries that unite and flow as the Thames into Long Island Sound, past New London and Groton. The Quinebaug doesn't seem like much of a river, but the petition respecting a division, submitted to the General Court by citizens of what was to be Canterbury, complained of "a long labarynth [sic] of difficulties by reason of a tedious river that is between us and them." The historian of the county speaks of "the difficulty of crossing the formidable Quinebaug in winter and high water." Many early bridges were carried away by ice or flood. The foremost problem it presented was the impracticability of maintaining a common church and support-ing one minister, as one community was likely to be shut off from its facilities much of the time. The annual upstream run of shad and salmon was so vital to the river towns that later in the century the construction of mill dams was an issue for litigation and intense local political strife. There were lesser streams which the town had to bridge also—Little River and Rowland's Brook.

The settlement of the boundaries of the new town was not harmonious. The county historian says that they "maintained an incessant border warfare . . . and many acts of Border-ruffianism" occurred on both sides, involving not only constant litigation but the pillaging of crops and timber and pulling down of fences. The contentious factions denounced each other in such bombastic Biblical terms as "the Great Troubler of Israel." The townspeople of Prudence's time, who bore the family names of those of a century earlier, were still a people who could work themselves into high dudgeon and extreme actions.

Not only material things agitated them. The history of the Congregational church was tempestuous. In one of the peri-odic waves of revivalistic passion that swept across the colonies in the eighteenth century, as they would continue to do in the growing United States for another hundred years, a large part of Canterbury's congregation found itself in rebellious dissent from the Consociation, the Connecticut orthodoxy, defying church authority and encouraging lay ministries. A correspond-ent reported in the *Boston Gazette*:

Dec. 16, 1742. Canterbury is in worse confusion than ever. Their minister has left them, and they grow more noisy and boisterous so that they can get no minister to preach to them yet. Colonel Dyer exerted his authority among them on the Lord's Day, endeavoring to still them when many were ex-

horting and making a great hubbub, and ordered the con-
stable to do his office, but they replied, "Get thee behind
me, Satan!" and the noise and tumult increased to such a
degree, for above an hour, that the exhorter could not begin
his exercise. Lawyer Paine [Elisha, whose presumed kinsman, another Elisha, erected the house that was to become
Prudence's school] has set up for a preacher . . . and makes
it his business to go from house to house and town to town
to gain proselytes to this new religion [as the orthodox called
the separatist movement]. Consequences are much feared.

One of the consequences was that lawyer-preacher Paine
went to jail, which he complained was the dirtiest he ever saw.
President Timothy Dwight of Yale, in his published *Travels,*
reports that Canterbury in the 1780's had difficulty in keeping
clergy and was afflicted by declining morals and dissension. By
Prudence's day the religious disputes which had raged sporadi-
cally for decades had subsided, but she became the cause of
renewed tumult in the house of the Lord.

The declining morals that Timothy Dwight remarked had
perhaps slipped still further when, in the next century, the
Reverend Asa Meech was called to the unquiet pulpit of Canterbury in 1812. He smote sin hip and thigh. As the county
historian observes:

"The horse-racing at Butts' Bridge race-course, the revelries at Masonic Hall, the all-night dances and promiscuous
frolicking, could hardly . . . escape reprobation. And if while
denouncing amusements as sins he limited the chances of ob-
taining forgiveness to 'about one in a million,' the Canterbury
people might be pardoned for adopting the conclusion of the
old negro upon a similar close calculation—'If only so few are
to be saved I think we had better not putter any more about
them.' "

The economy of Canterbury was based on farms, orchards,
and animal husbandry. But it included taverns (the village was

at the crossing of two major turnpikes, which, it should be remembered, were toll roads), grist mills, sawmills, tanneries, blacksmithies, cooperages, potash works, wool-carding mills, pottery kilns, hatmaking, and cloth-dressing. Captain Joseph Simms, near the Green, made and sold black woolen hats good for a lifetime, and he shipped them far away as well. There were six or eight stores on the Green—more than today by far. The town boasted even Abel Brewster's jewelry store. Lawyers and physicians, with clergy, were the chief professional men; but Canterbury, as we have seen, was a hot spot for ministers. There was a Masonic lodge where alleged "revelries" were held.

From about 1770, Canterbury's public schools were augmented by private schools. A public library was established in 1771 but its descendent of today is in evident decline. In 1796 a certain John Adams opened on the Green a school which flourished for quite a long time—a period that may have been the town's apex—and attracted students from some distance. Adams was genuinely devoted to aiding and guiding youth and helped many students. One such was a certain impoverished and physically handicapped Rinaldo Burleigh, of Ashford, who lived to become the father of six remarkable sons—one of whom, Charles C. Burleigh, was to play a large role in the affair of Prudence Crandall, while his brother William Henry taught in her school.

Other good things came out of Canterbury. Moses Cleveland (originally spelled Cleaveland) was born there in 1754, went to Yale, served with Washington, went to the Western Reserve which was a Connecticut jurisdiction, and was the principle founder of a settlement on the shores of Lake Erie that was later named Cleveland. He was of such swarthy complexion that when he was in the wilds, Indians often thought him one of themselves.

Jonathan Carver was brought to Canterbury as an eight-year-old child, in 1718. He grew up and married there. After the French and Indian Wars he made one of the important pioneer journeys westward across the northern tier. He went to England shortly before the War for Independence, settled for life, and there wrote his *Travels in Interior Parts of America* (1778).

The Christian names that run through town records for several generations, from the founding to Prudence's times, reflect the intense Bible-rootedness of these people: Nehemiah, Ebenezer, Hezekiah, Jedidiah, Isaiah, Ezekiel, Shubael, Solomon, Abijah, Silas, Elisha, Joshua, Moses, Asa, Seth, Abraham, Ahaziah, Ezra, Gideon—they are like a roll call of old Israel. David, though that name can be found, was not in wide use then, presumably because Puritans were too mindful of the murder and adultery committed by that great and beloved king, psalmist, and servant of God. There were of course hosts of other such names, including many which our present generations have largely forgotten are Biblical: John, Daniel, Samuel, Joseph, James.

The family names are remarkably persistent, among them: Fitch, Paine (or Payne), Adams, Johnson, Brown, Spalding, Woodward, Ensworth, Frost, Cleveland, Estabrook. There are some pleasing combinations: Jabez Utter, Eliphalet Dyer, Jedidiah Elderkin, Abiel Abbott, and Ebenezer Devotion, Jr. Many of these long-established names of the community figure largely in Prudence's case. They had also figured largely in the town's history as selectmen, town clerks, fence-viewers, magistrates, overseers of the poor, or justices of the peace.

Such were the people of Canterbury, diligent, determined to have and hold what they thought was theirs, God-fearing but theologically contentious, reasonably virtuous but overly persuaded of their virtue.

Altogether, a sense of the ambience of the Quinebaug valley and such a town as Canterbury can be found in the romantic prose of *Twice Married*, a piece of sentimental, idyllic, pious fiction by a contemporary of Prudence. The author speaks of the river, "flowing smoothly along, over a bed of white sand and pebbles, through level, green meadows, and between low, sloping banks, fringed with drooping willows. . . . The range of hills that form the western limits of the valley presents a bold front . . . hidden for half the year by . . . the chestnut woods . . . but the acclivity of the eastern hills is a gentle slope of fertile land, divided by intersecting walls and fences into fields and meadows, and thickly dotted with white farmhouses, orchards, and clumps of walnuts and shade-trees."

The road "is bordered by low rows of umbrageous maples, while here and there, by the road-side, a stately elm towers aloft into the air, sheltering a snug farm-house and its shady, green, front door-yard, beneath its spreading branches.

"About midway, on a gentle swell of land, a spur of the eastern hills, round which the loitering river makes a sweeping bend, the trees are more thickly planted, and at a little distance the place resembles a grove of elms and buttonwoods. But glimpses of white dwellings peeping out from among the dense foliage, and a slim spire, surmounted by a gilded ball and vane, rising over all, reveal the spot where the village . . . stands, almost hidden among the trees."

That is fiction, but it describes well the Canterbury country at that time. The author's name presents a tantalizing coincidence. He was Calvin Wheeler Philleo, an attorney. Prudence, just before the close of the Canterbury case, married a Reverend Calvin Philleo, a Baptist minister from Ithaca, New York. One longs to see a link here, but if it exists, as it may, archivists and genealogists have yet to document it.

[CHAPTER VII]

The Professionals

THE ANTI-PRUDENCE FACTION IN CANTERBURY NEVER HAD A
chance, in the long view. They were in the wrong, although
they did have some understandable grievances. But they were
up against do-good professionals of the toughest grain, battle-
tested, ruthless infighters for moral causes.

Garrison, most prominent interferer-from-a-distance, believed, like Barry Goldwater, that extremism in the defense
of liberty is no vice, and moderation in the pursuit of freedom
is no virtue. Two years younger than Prudence, who so vener-
ated him (and also outlived him by ten years), he was born in
Newburyport, Massachusetts, in 1805, the son of a drunken
sea captain who deserted the family. After an apprenticeship,
the young William became a journeyman printer, working at
different times on a variety of New England papers. He also
became the kind of passionate Puritan reformer who flung himself zealously into a dozen causes and could lash himself into
moral fervor over rum, war, gambling, or Sabbath-breaking,
with little distinction among them. When the Quaker Benja-
min Lundy directed his eyes to the evil of slavery, that became
ever after Garrison's true ruling cause.

A well-known bust of Garrison resembles a latter-day
Brutus—patrician in looks for all his humble origins, intelligent, lofty, determined, and a man who could be led by ideal-
ism to drastic acts.

He was a harsh, sometimes careless partisan, whose rash
charges once got him convicted and imprisoned for libel.

Arthur Tappan got him released. Soon after that, late in 1830, Garrison founded *The Liberator* with a partner, Isaac Knapp. The first issue, of January 1, 1831, carried his famous defiant cry: "I am in earnest—I will not equivocate—I will not excuse —I will not retreat a single inch—and I WILL BE HEARD." (When I was a youth those words gave me a heady lift of spirit. Today they tend to depress me. They are the words of a fanatic; and fanatics, even in just causes, are dangerous men). Once Garrison was led through the streets of Boston with a halter around his neck by an angry pro-slavery mob, and was jailed for his own protection by the mayor, who had rescued him. He proved his fearlessness time and again, showing himself to be one of those who, in Emerson's words, "rise refreshed on hearing a threat." For a time Garrison had to leave Boston till the place cooled down.

In the years following the Canterbury events Garrison repeatedly won notoriety. He was an outright disunionist, and from 1841 until civil war came, he constantly advocated the secession of all nonslaveholding states from the Union. He wrote and forced through the New-England Anti-Slavery Society a resolution denouncing the United States Constitution as "a covenant with death and an agreement with hell," calling for its annulment. On July 4, in Framingham, Massachusetts, he burned the Constitution publicly and proclaimed, with a curious anticipation of John Wilkes Booth, "So perish all compromises with tyranny!" He would be at home in the moods of today.

He was at his best in his insistence that all men should remember those in bonds as bound with them:

"It is the lowness of their estate, in the estimation of the world, which exalts them in my eyes. It is the distance which separates them from the blessings and privileges of society, which brings them so closely to my affections. It is the unmerited scorn, reproach and persecution of their persons, by those whose complexion *is* colored like my own, that command for them my sympathy and respect. It is the fewness of their friends, and the great number of their enemies, that induce me to stand forth in their defence."

Under his abrasive personality, the Abolition movement shattered into splinter fragments in the manner of modern left-wing parties. Anyone whose views deviated in the slightest from his orthodoxy, Garrison peremptorily read out of the movement. Harriet Beecher Stowe once wrote him, demanding: "Where is this work of excommunication to end?" He was a re- markable man, influential, in many respects admirable, in many ways deplorable and impossible; a man of a type that might be called the unscrupulous idealist, and who might have done well to pray, in words of poet Chad Walsh: "Forgive us our virtues, as we forgive those who are virtuous against us."

After the Canterbury town meeting, Garrison published the account sent him by Henry Benson, but embellished it with the headline: "HEATHENISM OUTDONE." He also wrote an introductory comment: "We put the names of the principal disturbers [by which he meant Judson and company] in black letter—black as the infamy which will attach to them as long as there exists any recollection of the wrongs of the colored race. To colonize these shameless enemies of their species in some desert country would be a relief and blessing to society. This scandalous excitement is one of the genuine flowers of the colonization garden." Of "colonization" we shall hear more, later.

Relatively mild for Garrison, this was nonetheless felt keenly by its targets in Canterbury. They were stung especially by the bold black letters in which their names were featured. Henry Benson wrote, "Your remarks in the last *Liberator* were awfully cutting."

Prudence herself, who had exhibited a budding talent for cutting remarks, was moved to write Garrison to cool it: "Per- mit me to entreat you to handle the prejudices of the people of Canterbury with all the *mildness* possible, as everything severe tends merely to heighten the flame of malignity amongst them. 'Soft words turn away wrath, but grievous words stir up anger.' Mr. May and many others of your warm-hearted friends feel very much on this subject, and it is our opinion that you and the cause will gain many friends in this town and vicinity if you treat the matter with perfect mildness." There the true Quaker spirit spoke in Prudence.

Samuel May said in a footnote to an open letter to Andrew T. Judson: "I respect and love Mr. Garrison's fervent devotion to the cause of the oppressed, and his fearlessness in reproving the oppressors; but no one can disapprove, more than I do, the harshness of his epithets, and the bitterness of his invectives." Arnold Buffum a few years later also broke with Garrison over his radical postures.

But the angry worthies of Canterbury, once they had seen Garrison in action, knew they were in a fight with a formidable and self-righteous distant opponent who didn't give a damn about their local concerns.

Garrison, who about a year later married one of the Benson girls, came to Brooklyn shortly after the town meeting and the subsequent opening of Prudence's school. He stayed with the Bensons and preached on a Sunday evening in Samuel May's pulpit. Prudence and Almira came up to hear him. He remarked: "She is a wonderful woman, as undaunted as if she had the whole world on her side." And one of his friends, the Reverend Simeon Jocelyn of New Haven, wrote him: "Miss C. has no doubt more praying friends in the United States drawn to her by her persecutions than the whole number of the population of Canterbury. . . . She is a noble soul."

The knowledge that their alien adversary was holding forth in Brooklyn had enraged the Canterburians. Garrison reported receiving a letter from Prudence, a few days later, "in which she stated that I had not left Brooklyn more than half an hour before a sheriff from Canterbury drove up to the door of Mr. Benson at full speed, having five writs against me from

Andrew T. Judson and company; and finding that I had gone, he pursued after me for several miles, but had to give up the chase."

"Our friend May," as Garrison called him, was a man of much softer speech and tactful action but of no less firm principles. We have seen in his deft management of the arrest of Prudence that he was a professional in using action and words for maximum propaganda effect and, at the least, did not scruple to exaggerate on what seemed to him the side of the angels.

The man who emerges from the *Memoir of Samuel Joseph May* and the diary pages incorporated in it, and from his book *Some Recollections of Our Anti-Slavery Conflict*, is a likable, gentle, kind, quietly courageous person. His portrait shows firm, pleasant features, the mouth suggesting determination but also generosity. He wore a fringe of whiskers beneath the chin, flaring into mutton chops at the sides, which whitened early while hair and eyebrows remained darker.

Born in 1797, called a "puny, frail" child, he had a traumatic shock at about four years of age, when his brother Edward, two years older, was fatally impaled in the armpit by a splintered chair post which broke as the boy was climbing on it, from which wound he bled to death. Samuel had a dream of an angelic visitation from his lost brother, a child's variation on the dream of Jacob and the angels, and May attributed his conviction of the immortality of the soul to this vision.

Childhood experiences with a bright and cheerful Negro child in school, and with a black woman who kindly helped young Samuel when he hurt himself, began his disposition of good will toward those who suffered because they were "guilty of a skin not colored like our own."

He was graduated from Harvard in 1817, already determined to make the ministry his calling. He was influenced toward the new Unitarianism by Dr. William Ellery Channing, whom the irreverent sometimes called the Unitarian Pope.

May became involved in many types of reform, from temperance movements to the abolition of corporal punishment. He formed a "Cold Water Army" of children to crusade against liquor. But abolition of slavery, as the overwhelming moral struggle of the age, commanded his greatest energies.

May's friends said of him, "His heart always overflowed with the milk of human kindness and his whole aim and desire was to make his fellow men better and happier," and "everyone who met him was drawn toward him." We do not necessarily love those who want to make us happier, or especially those who want to make us better—as if that were possible. May was mobbed five times at meetings in various New England states. But even enemies acknowledged his kindliness. At a time when Abolitionists were about as popular with many people as Black Panthers are today, one opponent conceded of May, "I have got to give up trying to hate that man."

There were those who called May Christlike. As a Unitarian in his time he sometimes found even members of that liberal, anti-Calvinist church movement "dogmatic." He spoke of "the divinity of Christ" but did not mean by that a literal, Trinitarian sonship. Yet the phrase "the Lord Jesus Christ" was common in his speech and writing. He had exchanged more absolute creeds for what he called a "Covenant which set forth only the simple, great doctrines of Christ and his apostles which all Christians of every denomination acknowledge they taught." His spirit was ecumenical. In his late years he was presented with a gold-headed cane by Roman Catholics of Syracuse, New York, for his aid in founding St. Mary's Hospital, to be run by the Sisters of Charity on nonsectarian principles.

The young minister came first to Brooklyn, Connecticut, in the winter of 1821 to supply only temporarily the pulpit of its first Unitarian church. Like nearby Canterbury, Brooklyn had been torn by fierce theological battles, when many of its Congregationalists split off from the body of Connecticut church orthodoxy, known as the Consociation. These dissenters had been persecuted in petty but hurtful ways. May proved to be a good healer of community bitterness. His congregation greatly wanted him to stay. May decided against it, partly on advice from his Boston and Cambridge friends and mentors, but about a year later, responding to renewed pleas and visitations, he consented to return there for a year's trial, which lengthened into a fourteen-year pastorate. Among the duties he took upon himself, to explain the Unitarian doctrines to still suspicious neighbors, was publication of a little paper called *The Liberal Christian,* which won him the respect and friendship of many, even if they did not all join his church.

Interested always in education, May invited the philosopher-innovator Bronson Alcott to visit him. Immediate admiring friendship soon became a family tie, for May's sister Abigail, then living with him in Brooklyn, married Alcott, becoming the mother of Louisa May Alcott, who wrote *Little Women.*

George Benson, a wealthy retired merchant of Providence, had come to dwell in Brooklyn. Some of the large family of Bensons were Quakers, others joined May's church. As we have seen, the sons, George and Henry, became participants in the Canterbury affair, and their sister Mary shared Prudence's night in the "murderer's cell" of the Brooklyn jail. Another Benson daughter, Helen, married William Lloyd Garrison in 1834.

May himself set down in *Recollections of Our Anti-Slavery Conflict* (1869) one of the most authoritative chronicles of the Canterbury struggle, of which he said, quoting Aeneas, "All of which I saw, and part of which I was."

Arthur Tappan, whom Prudence had visited in New York, who had supported an abortive project for a Negro college in New Haven, and who would shortly appear on the Canterbury scene, was another of the forceful professionals. He was born in 1786, son of a gold and silversmith, in Northampton, Mas-, sachusetts. The father also dealt in drygoods, and Arthur was to progress from clerkship in that line to rank as one of the foremost merchants of his day. In the strong, benevolent face, with white hair and beard, bushy brows and jutting nose, per- haps the stamp of the merchant is the tight mouth—actually belying his generous nature. His mother had commended to him the motto: "Dare to be singular."

On leaving home, Tappan clerked in the Boston store of Sewall and Salisbury. The Mays were connections of the Se- walls and for a time the youthful clerk boarded in the home of Samuel May's parents; thus the paths of these two co-laborers for abolition had crossed in former days. Tappan was some eleven years the elder and May would have been merely an infant. Tappan attended Dr. Channing's church. An uncle, Dr. David Tappan, was a professor of divinity at Harvard.

Arthur's first independent store was in Montreal, a busi- ness arbitrarily terminated by the War of 1812. In 1815 he established the drygoods store of Arthur Tappan & Co. in New York. He built up a volume of trade amounting to half a million a year, then a very large sum. In those years, also, he joined the Presbyterian Church. As a businessman he was said to have "two fixed principles: Never to have a chair in his office for visitors, and always to place a fixed price (which he made as low as possible) on all his goods." Ascetically abstemious, he took a cracker and a tumbler of water for lunch. He became a general philanthropist, supporting the Magdalen Society for fallen women, and the movements against liquor and tobacco. The widespread support of the temperance cause which we observe among these men cannot be understood by one who does not know that drunkenness was a major social problem, indeed disaster, in the United States during much of the nine- teenth century. Hogarthian "Gin Row" scenes were common in American cities.

Tappan, like many other antislavery people, at first sup-

ported the American Colonization Society, of which we shall
say more later, but soon came to see its true nature and became
its enemy. He contributed generously to all genuine antislavery
causes, actions, and publications while he possessed his wealth.
He suffered for it, also. In 1834 and 1835 his store in Pearl
Street, Hanover Square, was vandalized several times by pro-
slavery assailants. Tappan had to employ musket-carrying
guards to protect it. The house of his brother Lewis, his associate in all his causes, was set afire.

Southern merchants with whom he had done a large trade
boycotted him, as did many individual patrons in the north
who despised his principles. Some Southern attorneys refused
to conduct legal processes against Southern debtors in default
to Tappan. Extremist Southerners offered $50,000 for Tappan's
head, and he remarked: "If that sum is placed in the New
York Bank, I may possibly think of giving myself up." Once
at a prayer meeting in the First Presbyterian Church of Brooklyn, New York, Tappan introduced an intercession for slaves
into a public prayer, and was "scraped down" for it—the
phrase of dissidents in the congregation who interrupted him
with protests, causing him to sit down. Several of New York's
bankers and financiers, with whom Tappan had extensive
transactions and enjoyed high credit rating, warned him that
in the event of any financial setbacks, his antislavery activities
would prevent his receiving aid.

It happened. The store suffered from general business
reverses after the economic crash of 1837. Tappan was further
undone by the rashness of his own generosity; entering a real
estate operation simply to help a friend, he found himself
caught in a collapsing enterprise. The philanthropist and social
reformer had taken precedence over the businessman in Tappan's life. In 1840 he was forced to enter into bankruptcy. His
personal standing was still so high that another merchant, not
in sympathy with the Abolition movement, said, "If Arthur
Tappan will allow his name to be put up on my store, and sit

in an arm-chair in my counting room, I will pay him $3,000 a year"—a much more impressive sum than it sounds today, perhaps by a factor of ten.

As early as 1828, Tappan had purchased the former Morse family house, in New Haven, from Samuel F. B. Morse, the painter and inventor of the telegraph. There Tappan spent his own last years, in dignity but no longer able to dispense great sums for causes in which he believed. But during the Canterbury affair, when the lean years had not yet overtaken him, Tappan underwrote *The Unionist*—a paper founded to present Prudence's case—and met many other expenses of the cause, which May noted with gratitude ran to something more than six hundred dollars.

Such were some of the men from "abroad" who rallied to Prudence Crandall in Canterbury and ultimately took the management of the case from her hands.

CHAPTER VIII

A Larger Context

WE HAVE SEEN GARRISON, IN EXPRESSING HIS CONCERN THAT "Miss Crandall must be sustained at all hazards," refer to "The New Haven excitement" which had "furnished a bad precedent."

In 1831, a convention of free colored people was held in Philadelphia. Delegates from several states convened, together with many white friends, to consider broad questions about the welfare of free Negroes. All agreed that education, especially of practical and mechanical kinds, was an urgent need. It was decided to set up, in New Haven, Connecticut, what they described as "a Collegiate school on the manual labor system" to "cultivate habits of industry" and "obtain a useful *Mechanical* or *agricultural* profession."

New Haven was selected because of its reputation as an enlightened community, with a record of good will toward colored people. It also had trade links with the British West Indies where, it was believed, slaves were soon to be emancipated, a policy whose example New Haven might help spread.

It was felt that the proximity of Yale College would be an advantage, that some of its professors might be willing to lecture occasionally at the Negro college and otherwise aid its work. The Reverend Simeon S. Jocelyn, of New Haven, was one of the initiators of the project, and another backer was Arthur Tappan, who bought land for the college and also pledged cash contributions.

When the plan became public, in September of 1831, the

sponsors received a rude shock. A wave of opposition arose. Nat Turner's bloody slave revolt had just previously agitated the fears of slaveowners in the South and of all persons in the North who looked upon black men with distaste or distrust.

Moreover, the Reverend Mr. Jocelyn wrote to Garrison: "We have touched the very *quick* of oppression simply by calling the institution a *College*. Our enemies all over the country start at the name. Why? Because it carries the assurance of equality with it. We would not lose the name on any account." Even at Yale College there was unanticipated resistance, though some professors were sympathetic to the Negroes. Yale had a large proportion of Southern students, alumni, and benefactors, and it was feared the College would suffer by proximity to such a place of black education as proposed.

"A negro college by the side of Yale College!" "The City of Elms disgraced for ever!" "It must not and shall not be!" In one contemporary account such were said to be "popular cries." We doubt they ever got cried, but they did get printed, and they achieved their purpose.

On the tenth of September, a New Haven town meeting was held, at which the Mayor and the City Council presented strong resolutions. Their key themes were that "the propagation of sentiments favorable to the immediate emancipation of slaves, in disregard of the civil institutions of the States in which they belong, and as auxilliary thereto, the contemporaneous founding of Colleges for educating Colored People, is an unwarrantable and dangerous interference with the internal concerns of other States and ought to be discouraged. . . .

"And Whereas in the opinion of this Meeting, Yale College, the institutions for the education of females, and the other schools, already existing in this City, are important to the community and the general interests of science, and as such have been deservedly patronized by the public, and the establishment of a College in the same place to educate the Colored population is incompatible with the prosperity, if not the existence of the present institutions of learning, and will be destructive of the best interests of the City: and believing as we do, that if the establishment of such a College in any part of the Country were deemed expedient, it should never be imposed on any community without their consent,—Therefore; Resolved . . . that we will resist the establishment of the proposed College in this place, by every lawful means."

Both sides in the Canterbury dispute saw parallels between the New Haven case and their smaller one. Though Canterbury was a mere village compared to New Haven, and though Prudence's intended school was of vastly smaller scale, the underlying attitudes and principles were the same. The New Haven project was dropped because of the intensity of feeling expressed against it. Clearly Prudence's opponents assumed that the same thing would happen with hers; on the precedent, it was a reasonable assumption. That was what worried Garrison and the other professional Abolitionists.

The lines were clear: to those who disliked or feared the Negro, their education meant equality and ultimately amalgamation of the races. By Negroes, and those concerned for their advancement, education was seen as the first necessity of freedom and self-respecting independence. The Negro's capacity for such a way of life was not in doubt. The plight of free Negroes was often difficult, but this was long before the age of urban black ghettoes and the sloth, despair, and criminality that ghetto poverty breeds in some. A Yale professor called it "delightful to see so many of our colored people living in neat and comfortable dwellings furnished in decent taste, and sufficient fulness: thus indicating sobriety, industry, and self-respect— to see their children in clean attire, hastening of a Sabbath morning to the Sunday-school; and other days, with cheerful intelligent faces, seeking the common school."

There was yet another factor behind the rancor of some of the leading men of Canterbury, especially Andrew T. Judson. Theirs was the special wrath and frustration of men who regarded themselves as respectable friends of the colored people, upon finding themselves suddenly cast as monsters and oppressors. Judson was a member, or at least a sympathizer, of the American Colonization Society, which leads us to the melancholy fact of a savage quarrel between two large groups of citizens, throughout the country, each of whom claimed to be the principal friends of the black man.

The American Colonization Society was organized in 1816 in Washington. Henry Clay presided over the first meeting—somewhat baleful auspices! As early as that time, the new republic being yet in its infancy, there was concern not just about slavery among those who considered it wrong (which included Washington, Jefferson, and Madison, each of whom held slaves but wished to see the practice ended), but also there was worry about the increasing number of free Negroes. Southern slaveholders considered free Negroes in their midst an inherent threat to the system, an inflammatory example, and in some cases a source of agitation among slaves. In the North, where many free Negroes settled, there were fears ranging from economic competition among the poorer classes of whites to visions among upper classes of amalgamation by intermarriage. It was not surprising, therefore, that prominent men in both North and South agreed that something should be done about the free Negro and that the ideal something was that he should be shipped back to Africa.

The American Colonization Society raised funds and purchased a large tract of land on the west coast of Africa. To this place it proposed to send any free Negroes who would voluntarily return to the continent of their ancestors—withal one which none of them had ever seen. The country was called Liberia; its principal city and capital was named Monrovia, in honor of President Monroe, who had given the venture his encouragement. The Society administered Liberia as a private enclave until 1847, at which time it was proclaimed an independent republic—the first of its kind in black Africa.

In the early years of the Colonization Society, many people who desired the abolition of slavery joined the Society, believing that it was of benefit to colored people and would also advance Christian missions in Africa. But it was never intended that slaves be freed and sent there. When a few slaveholders occasionally released a troublesome slave on the condition that he go to Liberia, it was seen that even the voluntary aspect of the migrations was compromised. Being sent to Liberia, where conditions were hard and disease and poverty were rife, could be analogous to a Russian being sent to Siberia. Perceiving, at last, that Colonization was essentially a force for the protection of slavery, all who hated slavery withdrew from it. The Abolition movement then emerged, the foremost of many leaders in it being William Lloyd Garrison. Abolitionists waged unremitting war upon the Colonization Society, denouncing it as hypocritical and actively harmful to the welfare of Negroes, free or slave.

As for Negroes themselves, a convention of free people of color, meeting in Philadelphia in January, 1817, only months after the promulgation of the Colonizationists' program and their invitation to go to Africa, passed resolutions which said in part:

> We have no wish to separate from our present homes for any purpose whatever. Contented with our present situation and condition, we are not desirous of increasing their prosperity but by honest efforts, and by the use of those opportunities for their improvement, which the constitution and the laws allow to all. It is, therefore, with painful solicitude and sorrowing regret, we have seen a plan for colonizing the free people of color of the United States, on the coast of Africa. . . . let not a purpose be assisted which will stay the cause of the entire abolition of slavery in the United States, and

which may defeat it altogether; which proffers to those who do not ask for them, *benefits,* but which they consider *injuries,* and which must insure to the multitudes, whose prayers can only reach you through us, *misery, sufferings, and perpetual slavery.*

Two free black men of Middletown, Connecticut, asked: "Why should we leave this land, so dearly bought by the blood, groans and tears of our fathers? Truly this is our home, here let us live and here let us die."

It was this perceptive unequivocal rejection of Colonization by articulate and educated free black men that made Garrison and the other outright Abolitionists see the falseness of its premises.

The Fifteenth Annual Report of the Colonization Society makes its view of the blacks explicit—the italics and capital letters are theirs:

Causes beyond the control of the human will must prevent their ever rising to equality with the white. . . . The managers consider it clear, that causes exist, and are operating, to prevent their improvement and elevation to any considerable extent, as a class, in this country, which are fixed, not only beyond the control of the friends of humanity, BUT OF ANY HUMAN POWER. Christianity cannot do for them here, what it will do for them in Africa. This is not the fault of the colored man, *nor of the white man,* nor of Christianity; but it is AN ORDINATION OF PROVIDENCE, and *no more to be changed than the laws of nature.*

In short, it was God's fault.

This wish that the blacks who had been brought unwillingly from Africa could be sent back, willingly or unwillingly, was in part the wish that they had never been brought here in the first place. No one who sensed the ultimate tragedy and grim problems of slavery within the nation, even if he had no particular moral aversion to it, could help but wish the blacks could be sent away. On the other hand, remember that within the black community itself, long after slavery had been abolished, there have been periodic waves of a desire to go back to Africa. Marcus Garvey led such a movement, in Harlem, in the years following World War I. Black separatism now shows itself in a variety of forms among black militants, though the return to Africa is no longer the goal of separatist movements, some of which now desire, at the least, black statehood somewhere within the confines of the United States.

We don't know whether or not Judson had actively supported Colonization before the Crandall case—May doubted it —but he was later made agent of the Windham County Colonization Society and a life member, as was his colleague on the Garrison black-letter list, Dr. Harris.

Following the town meeting, Judson and the other town officials prepared a formal address to the Colonization Society, appealing for its moral support, and sounding again those fears of colored invasion and amalgamation which underlay the whole idea of sending the blacks back where they came from. "We appeal to the American Colonization Society . . . we appeal to every philanthropist, to every Christian—we appeal to the enlightened citizens of our native State and the friends of our country; and in making that appeal we assure them all that they may rely upon the facts here stated." These "facts" included the assertion that the "school was to become an auxiliary in the work of *immediate abolition*," adding, "once open this door, and New England will become the Liberia of America." Thus there was some truth in Garrison's fierce description of the Canterbury case as "one of the genuine flowers of the colonization garden."

At the time of the Canterbury case, there were some twenty slaves in the whole state of Connecticut, and some eight thousand free Negroes. That was close to the maximum number of free Negroes in the state before the Civil War. Slaves had reached their highest number in the state around 1774, with something over six thousand, which number had diminished steadily. The latest report of any slaves there is in 1848.

Among the ironies of the New Haven and Canterbury cases, as many pointed out, was the fact that Connecticut had always prided itself on a tradition of liberty. It had an extensive network of routes and way stations in the Underground Railroad system. Over the years there were some eighty-six active agents of that clandestine escape network in the state as a whole. Windham County had thirteen, which includes an otherwise unspecified "Crandall" in Canterbury (perhaps it was Pardon, but the subject does not arise in the records of Prudence), and several other actors in this story: Samuel May, George Benson, and Charles Burleigh. Horatio Strother, chronicler of *The Underground Railroad in Connecticut*, calls New Haven the fugitives' "gateway from the sea." Farmington, close to Hartford, he calls the "Grand Central Station" because so many routes converged there. By 1837, Connecticut had as many as thirty-nine Anti-Slavery Societies, a few of which were subclassified as "male" or "female" or even "colored."

CHAPTER IX

The Unionist

THE PASSAGE OF THE "BLACK LAW" MADE CLEAR THAT THE feelings of Prudence's opponents in Canterbury represented no particular villainy of that community but an aspect of human nature at large. These were not bad men, but to paraphrase Shaw's *Saint Joan,* as honest a lot of poor fools as ever persecuted their betters—more truly, their peers. Prudence and company were not inherently *better* than their adversaries, but they were oriented differently and the consensus of conscience, historically, regards their direction as better. "We should not want a nigger school on *our* common," was said by many persons in other Connecticut towns. And though color easily induced polarization into "we" and "they," there was precedent in Connecticut's legislative history for the attempt to exclude unwanted persons and activities. The historian of Windham County says: "Ninety years before when asked by the standing clergy and churches to devise some means for keeping out irregular preachers and itinerants, their predecessors had enacted that a minister from out of the State preaching without the invitation of a stated minister or society should be sent like a vagrant by warrant out of the bounds of the Colony."

When the Assembly was deliberating its measure against Prudence, gentle Pardon Crandall sent a printed plea to the lawmakers not to "pass any act that will curtail or destroy any of the rights of the free people of this State or other States whether they are white or black."

In the flush of his satisfaction over the law, Andrew Judson rubbed it in to the old Quaker: "Mr. Crandall, when you sent your printed paper to the General Assembly, you did not injure us; it helped very much in getting the bill through. When they received it every man clinched his fist, and the chairman of the committee sat down and doubled the penalty. Members of the Legislature said to me—'If this law does not answer your purpose, let us know, and next year we will make you one that will.' "

In the next phase of the siege, pressure was concentrated on Pardon, whom they rightly assessed as a person of less native firmness, or non-Quakerish militancy, than his elder daughter. Two townsmen called on him to underscore that, as one aiding and assisting the school, he was himself liable to the harsh, doubling, redoubling, open-ended schedule of fines threatened in the law: ". . . if you go to your daughter's you are to be fined $100, for the first offence; $200 for the second, and double it every time; Mrs. Crandall, if you go there, you will be fined and your daughter Almira will be fined, and Mr. May and those gentlemen from Providence [the younger Bensons], if they come there will be fined at the same rate. And your daughter, the one that established the school for colored females, will be taken up the same way as for stealing a horse, or for burglary. Her property will not be taken but she will be put in jail, not having the liberty of the yard. There is no mercy to be shown about it!"

The father, distressed and appalled by what had engulfed them all, urged Prudence to yield to the overwhelming opposition and close the school. Her refusal could not have surprised him, and in spite of his fear and her rejection of his counsel, he continued to support her as best he could, to fetch water and other supplies.

Meanwhile, one aspect of Judson's challenge to May now loomed urgently: "Where will you get the means to carry on such a contest at law?" Here entered Arthur Tappan. Prudence had called on him on her trip to New York. He had followed the course of events through the pages of *The Liberator*. May says, "I was not then personally acquainted with him," which was true in spite of Tappan's early residence for a time with May's parents when Samuel was an infant. One day a letter arrived for May from the merchant. It expressed approval and admiration of the clergyman's tactics and added:

"This contest, in which you have been providentially called to engage, will be a serious, perhaps a violent one. It may be prolonged and very expensive. Nevertheless, it ought to be persisted in to the last. I venture to presume, sir, that you cannot well afford what it may cost. You ought not to be left, even if you are willing, to bear alone the pecuniary burden. I shall be most happy to give you all the help of this sort that you may need. Consider me your banker. Spare no necessary expense. Command the services of the ablest lawyers. See to it that this great case shall be thoroughly tried, cost what it may. I will cheerfully honor your drafts to enable you to defray that cost."

The grateful May, in one of the letters that began to pass between the men, exclaimed: "O that I could only leave home long enough to visit you! For I could tell you in an hour more things, that I wish you to know, than I can write in a week." A few days later he found Arthur Tappan, unannounced, at his door.

"Your last letter implied that you were in so much trouble I thought it best to come and see, and consider with you what it will be advisable for us to do."

After they had talked a while, Tappan took a horse and chaise and drove down to Canterbury to visit the school, returning some hours afterward highly impressed by the determination of pupils and teachers, and their persistent application to schoolwork amid the distractions of siege.

The strategists then concluded that the first need was a local press. The newspapers of all the surrounding towns, including Norwich, the largest, were unanimously hostile to Prudence. They closed even their letter columns to her partisans. In some instances it was simply their form of prudence. One small publisher whom May had helped to establish in business pled, apologetically, that to print anything in support of the school would be the ruin of him.

It was true that *The Liberator* covered the case extensively. It was also given notice in other sorts of "true-believer" papers, such as *The Emancipator* and *The Genius of Temperance*. But these were not local and reached only distant constituents already convinced.

Now Tappan asserted: "You are almost helpless without the press. You must issue a paper, publish it largely, send it to all the persons whom you know in the county and State, and to all the principal newspapers throughout the country. Many will subscribe for it and contribute otherwise to its support, and I will pay whatever more it may cost."

The two men went out immediately into the village of Brooklyn, to a printing shop that had failed. Its equipment and materials on hand—paper, ink, type—were enough for their needs. On the spot, Tappan contracted for the premises for a year. Within an hour the activist merchant had stepped onto the stagecoach in front of May's house, leaving the clergyman, somewhat bedazzled by the speed and scale of operations, to work out the details and find the hands to get the press going.

There must be someone engaged full time to edit it, which included writing a great deal of it, and to set the type, print it, and mail it. May had noticed an article denouncing the "Black Law" in *The Genius of Temperance*. Its author was Charles C. Burleigh of nearby Plainfield. The morning after Tappan's whirlwind trip, May drove to the farm of the elder Burleigh, parent of his prospective editor. May did not know this family, although he had once heard Charles Burleigh deliver a talk at a Colonization Society meeting. It was a Friday, in the midst of haying time, and the air was full of the fragrance of new-mown hay, the sweetest, freshest odor known to agriculture or any other pursuit of man except, perhaps, the baking of bread. Haying days are not a time to interrupt farmers, and Charles, though a law student, was in the fields aiding his family. At the house they demurred at the suggestion of sending for him. May pressed the point that his errand was one of those rare ones that might take precedence over haying. The word was sent out, and after a while C. C. Burleigh came in, sweating, covered with the chaff of his work, and with a week's growth of untrimmed beard.

To May the encounter summoned up Old Testament imagery: "I do not believe that Samuel of old saw, in the ruddy son of Jesse, as he came up from the sheepfold, the man whom the Lord would have him anoint, more clearly than I saw in C. C. Burleigh the man whom I should choose to be my assistant in that emergency. So soon as I had told him what I wanted of him his eye kindled as if eager for the conflict."

Still, a man does not lightly walk out of his father's field in mid-haying, even for good works. May pledged the money to hire another hand to replace him. Monday morning, July 14, 1833—a fine liberty-echoing date—Burleigh turned up in Brooklyn, took over the small press, and *The Unionist* was born.

The Burleighs were an extraordinary family. The father was Rinaldo Burleigh. The mother, the former Lydia Bradford, born in Canterbury, was a direct descendent of Governor William Bradford of Plymouth Plantation. Rinaldo had attended John Adams' school in Canterbury, was graduated from Yale College in 1803, the year of Prudence's birth, and became caught up, like his children after him, in the intellectually stimulating, reform-minded, but often eccentric currents of New England Transcendentalism and Abolitionism. He became principal of the Plainfield academy, but was forced out of education by the failure of his eyesight which was attributed, al-

most certainly wrongly, to excessive study. He resorted to
farming, aided at various times by all of his six sons, four of
whom became prominent in the antislavery movement.

The best known of them were Charles Calistus, whom May
had now recruited, George Shepard, and William Henry. The
latter two both were prolific though not distinguished poets,
generally using their versifying—which was all it was—in advancement of reform causes. But a natural eloquence and a
rhetoric unusually rich in images characterized them all. Rinaldo had not the means to give his sons the equivalent of his
education at Yale, but with their good minds and diligence
all educated themselves. William Henry later assisted Charles
in some of the work of *The Unionist* and also taught in Prudence's school—its only male teacher. For this he had rotten
eggs flung at him on the Canterbury streets.

C. C. when he took charge of *The Unionist,* had shaved the
rough beard May had observed as he came from the field. A few
years later, however, hair became one of the most conspicuous
aspects of Burleigh's rapidly flowering eccentricity. To look
ahead: in 1835 he was admitted to the bar, passing his ex-
aminations with distinction. At that point, he was diverted
from the fine career prospects that lay ahead of him by an
appeal, again reaching him through Samuel May, to go forth
on the antislavery lecture circuit.

May described the long silence, and the complex play of
emotion he could read in Burleigh's face at that time, as he
began a reflection that lasted a good part of an hour. Then,
his features brightening with commitment, Burleigh said, "This
is not what I expected or intended, but it is what I ought to
do."

He became known as the most formidable debater in the
Abolition movement. He worked much with Garrison, writing
for and sometimes helping to edit *The Liberator*. May called
him "single-minded, pure-hearted, conscientious, self-sacrific-
ing." But his peculiarity increased with his zeal, to an extent

WILLIAM LLOYD GARRISON. Portrait by William Swain, 1825.
Courtesy Professor Walter M. Merrill.

Arthur Tappan

ARTHUR TAPPAN in his later years. Engraved from a photograph, ca. 1862. Reproduced from *William Lloyd Garrison, 1805-1879: The Story of His Life Told by His Children.*

which even the admiring May believed impaired the effect of his abilities. He wore unusual clothing and let both hair and beard grow freely. Once he arrived at the home of an Abolitionist who had invited him to a town to lecture. He had not arrived on the stagecoach, as expected. When a knock was heard at the door, the children of the house rushed to answer it. "There stood a tall figure with long beard and ringlets, dusty with foot-travel, and carrying a pack of anti-slavery publications slung at the end of a rough staff resting on his shoulder. The first child to catch sight of him rushed back to the sitting-room crying: 'Oh, mother, mother! the Devil has come.'" So it often seemed to those who favored slavery or despised the blacks. But another image was more often conjured up by his appearance; he was much sought by painters as a model for the figure of Jesus.

But these exoticisms had not yet appeared in Charles C. Burleigh, then twenty-three, as he took up his duties in Brooklyn. *The Unionist* was issued weekly for almost two years, beginning August 1, 1833. It is not certain that publication was uninterruptedly regular. Little is known about the paper, for it has disappeared almost entirely. Only two copies of single issues are now known to exist. Volume 1, number 2, of Thursday, August 8, 1833, is in the library of the New-York Historical Society, where on first inquiry by this writer it could not be located, until one persistent staff member, seeing an easy pitfall, found it misfiled under Brooklyn, New York. The issue of September 5, 1833, is in the Library of the American Antiquarian Society, Worcester, Massachusetts.

The paper was printed as a single sheet, folded once to make four pages, slightly larger than a modern tabloid. Its subscription rate was $2.00 a year, in advance, for mail delivery; it could be picked up at the office for $1.50 a year. Though it was expressly concerned with the defense of Prudence, its prospectus asserted: "*The Unionist* will be the advocate of temperance, virtue and sound morality, and will pursue that course which a deep conviction of the truth of the sentiment contained in its motto points out." That motto was, "Righteousness Exalteth a Nation." The masthead figure was a printing press, with the ribbon banner: "The tyrants foe the peoples friend."

It is not recorded how the paper's name was chosen, but it seems clear that it was meant to emphasize the national implications of the Canterbury case and the Black Law. It stresses the Union as against the states, supporting the case of the uniformity of rights and the freedom of movement from state to state, for education or anything else.

Bluntly, *The Unionist* appears to have been a dull sheet, though no more so than all the other abolitionist and reform papers of the era, even *The Liberator*. They did not seem dull to their true believers, but almost nothing can bring them to life now. To have seen one or two of them is truly to have seen them all, except for their documentary value as a chronicle of movements.

For one thing, all of them resorted to a quantity of dreary filler material, pietistic, moralistic, sometimes patriotic-with-an-angle, reprinted incestuously from similar journals. Much of the front page of *The Unionist's* August 8 issue is filled by a Fourth of July oration unrelated to Prudence's case. The back page, as with other such papers, is "literary," given to bad poems and sententious prose; barren stuff, mainly. One must comb through the columns for the items that are the real occasion for the paper's being. It is impossible to say that this was uniformly true when only two issues out of something approaching one hundred survive, but the likelihood is strong. True, the September 5 issue, and evidently the one before it, carried a lengthy report of Prudence's trial, but only a few issues can have had so much substantial material to offer each week.

The prevailing style is heavy-handed and morally complacent. But again, this was the polemical manner of the period. It has its equivalents today, as in every time in which men have engaged in passionate quarrels over their visions of right or wrong, truth or heresy, justice or injustice. However dry these two surviving copies of *The Unionist* seem today, Prudence's cause had acquired a press, and it exerted an influence. That the case was becoming known far from home is seen in *The Unionist's* excerpts from newspaper comments from all over Connecticut, and from Vermont, Rhode Island, Massachusetts, New York, and Pennsylvania. Many such papers give exaggerated accounts of the outrage of Prudence's imprisonment in a murderer's cell—showing how successfully the propaganda effect of that ploy had been calculated.

To the credit of *The Unionist*, it did what few opposition papers would do—printed statements from the other side. A long joint letter from Andrew T. Judson and Rufus Adams is featured prominently in the August 8 issue. In it they protest:

> No one will say that she could not have given the bond on the spot. But it had been agreed before hand, by those who directed her what to do, that she should go to jail. She went and staid as long as suited her purposes, less than 24 hours, and then gave the bond. Some person has put in wide circulation, the story that she was confined in the cell of Watkins the murderer. This is part of the same contrivance to "get up more excitement!" She never was confined in the "murderer's cell." She was lodged in the debtor's room, where every accommodation was provided, both for her and *her friends*, whose visits were constant. She was confined nowhere else. It is said in justification of this untruth, that Watkins, some of the last days of his life, was taken out of his cell to receive the clergy and his friends, in the debtor's room, because it was more convenient.

That same letter included their vision of the sentiments and moral posture of themselves and their fellow townsmen:

We distinctly state to all who may feel an interest in this
matter, that we are not opposed to the education and kind
treatment of the colored people. It is not in the power of
any man, in truth, to say, that we have ever ill-treated a
person of color. We desire to see them free and happy. This
is the universal sentiment of the inhabitants of the town,
so far as we know it. Our schools admit colored children to
equal privileges, and we rejoice that they do so.

But then comes the crux of the matter—what is the tendency
of any given school? What will be taught there?

Those schools are all visited and are under the superintend-
ence of proper boards, excluding all danger, from the inculca-
tion of erroneous principles. The law now in force, makes
schools for foreign blacks subject to the assent of the civil
authority and select men of each town, so that it is an easy
matter to have such a school now, provided that board
could be satisfied that no pernicious principles are to be in-
culcated, and no danger could arise to the town or state. Is
not this right? Why should any person desire to force upon
any community, a school of any sort, against all their wishes?
Have the inhabitants no right to be heard in reference to the
location of such an institution among them, and more especially when they know the dangerous consequences to which
such measures would tend? Are the people of this State ready
to admit that the abolitionists, as they are called, are diffus-
ing sentiments and opinions consistent with the constitution
and the peace of society? Is there any individual in the
State of Connecticut who would feel willing to have such a
school, together with all the necessary evils, situated within
his own town or village? The answer will be, no. Then let
the same feeling be extended to us. This is the only way to
ascertain whether the town of Canterbury has done right or
wrong. The distinct objection which has been made by the
inhabitants of the town, to the location of this school within
its limits, consists in the dangerous tendency of the principles
pressed by the abolitionists wherever they go, in language

peculiar to themselves.—These principles are well understood, and it would be with deep regret, that any school should be established and continued, for their advancement, in a community where our friends are compelled to reside.

This is the best face of *The Unionist* and of all the supporters of Prudence. They would use every tactic of persuasion and propaganda. They would exaggerate to the verge of misrepresentation—as their opponents did—as most of us will do. But they had enough conviction of the strength of their case, and of their ability to present it, that they could open their columns to opponents whose arguments, they felt certain, could not pass the tests of close scrutiny or of time.

CHAPTER X

The County Trial

Prudence's case came to trial on August 23, 1833, at the Windham County Court, in Brooklyn. May remarked the irony that the court was "within a stone's throw of the house where lived and died General Israel Putnam, who, with his compatriots of 1776, perilled his life in defence of the self-evident truth that 'all men were created *equal*, and endowed by their Creator with the inalienable right to life, liberty, and the pursuit of happiness.'" How hard it was to decide who might claim that inalienable right will be seen in the arguments of counsel in the second and third trials. The first was concerned principally with establishing the charges and facts. It was in the second trial and subsequent appeal that the profound principles involved came most clamorously to the foreground.

The Honorable Joseph Eaton presided at the County Court. The prosecuting attorneys were Andrew T. Judson, Jonathan A. Welch, and I. Bulkley. On Arthur Tappan's advice, May had retained to defend Prudence men whom he regarded as "the three most distinguished members of the Connecticut bar": W. W. Ellsworth, Calvin Goddard, and Henry Strong. Of these three, William Wolcott Ellsworth was the commanding figure. He came of a notable family. His father, Oliver Ellsworth, had succeeded John Marshall to become second Chief Justice of the United States Supreme Court. W. W.'s twin brother, Henry Leavitt, was both lawyer and agriculturist, and held several important federal posts. He was mayor of Hartford when President Andrew Jackson appointed him commissioner of patents. Later he became known as the "father of the Department of Agriculture." Moving to Indiana, he was the first to see the value of America's prairie lands. Considered an eccentric for his belief in the future of agricultural machinery, he is said to have brought the first mowing machine to the prairies.

W. W. Ellsworth himself, at the time of Prudence's trial, was a United States Congressman from Connecticut. Later he served as governor, and afterwards, until retirement, as an associate judge of the state supreme court. He was tall, of imposing presence, looking, says the *Dictionary of American Biography*, like "an embodiment of a typical Connecticut Yankee, equally able to trade horses, make a political speech, and offer prayer." Prudence needed all his talents.

The first part of the trial consisted of the introduction of testimony by the prosecution to establish the fact that the school existed, that Miss Crandall "with force and arms did wilfully and knowingly harbor, board, and aid, and assist, in harboring and boarding certain colored persons." Those named as present for "instruction and teaching" were Theodosia Degrass, Ann Peterson, Ann Elizabeth Wilder, Ann Eliza Hammond, "and others whose names are unknown" (a legal formula for including all other students). The names of a few others turn up on some of the legal documents at various stages of the case: Catherine Ann Weldon, Mariah Robinson, G. C. Marshall. Spellings vary in the faded, brittle longhand documents. Probably there will never be a precise count or roll call of that brave band of "misses of color."

Technicalities were the most interesting aspect of the trial. From the start, Prudence's counsel conceded that she had broken the Black Law. Their case was to be based on a challenge of its constitutionality. Nevertheless, when the prosecution sought to place Ann Peterson, one of the Negro students, on the stand, "Mr. Ellsworth objected . . . on the ground that she could not testify without implicating herself. Mr. Welch read the clause of the Statute under which this prosecution was sustained, in which it was enacted that the pupils in a school kept contrary to the act might be compelled to testify. Mr. Ellsworth said that he denied altogether, the competency of the Legislature to compel a witness to testify, or to answer a question that might implicate him." This was to be an aspect of the general claim of unconstitutionality. Mr. Judson argued that the witness was not herself charged with any crime and therefore could not incriminate herself. Judge Eaton sustained him.

A series of questions was put to Ann Peterson: "Has Miss Crandall kept a school for Colored Misses not inhabitants of the State?" "Will you say whether the defendent has or has not instructed any person of color other than yourself, since the 10th of June last?" "With whom do you board?" Under Ellsworth's instructions she declined to answer. Two other students, Catherine Ann Weldon and Ann Eliza Hammond, were called to the stand and also refused to reply. The prosecutor reserved the right to move charges of contempt of court against them. Ann Eliza, who had previously been threatened with public whipping upon her naked body, was no more intimidated now than she had been then.

The Reverend Levi Kneeland, pastor of the Packerville Baptist Church, which had opened its doors to admit the Negro girls to worship, also invoked the Fifth Amendment in refusal to answer a number of questions. The judge and prosecution took a hard line with him and placed him in custody with the Sheriff for commitment to prison for contempt of court. A little later he was returned to the stand, at his own request, having been advised by Prudence's counsel that he could not incriminate himself and thus should testify. He acknowledged that he "had visited Miss Crandall's school twice . . . he had prayed in her school, and conversed with the girls on religious subjects . . . had taken meals at Miss Crandall's, and eaten with her pupils—he heard them recite their lessons."

Prudence's brother Hezekiah was called, and affirming rather than swearing, conceded that he knew his sister kept the school as charged. Eliza Glasko, a pupil who was a resident of Connecticut, had also declined to testify. When her arrest for contempt was put in motion, Ellsworth returned her to the stand and advised her to give evidence. She testified that some of her fellow students were from out of the state. As to the operation of the school, the instruction comprised "the ordinary branches . . . reading, writing, grammar; geography, &c. . . . the school was usually opened and closed with prayer—the scriptures were read and explained daily, in her school—some portions were committed to memory by the pupils, and considered a part of their education."

Thus at length the unchallenged facts were elicited and counsel proceeded to arguments. These turned fundamentally on a constitutional question. Were free Negroes citizens? The contention of the defense was that they were citizens, and thus enjoyed in Connecticut any essential rights, such as those to free movement and education, that they enjoyed in the states from which they came.

Ellsworth made the additional plea to the jury: "In order to convict my client, you, gentlemen, must find on your oaths that she has committed a crime. You may find that she has violated an act of the State legislature, but if you also find her protected by a higher power, it will be your duty to acquit."

Judson and his colleagues denied that free Negroes were citizens, claiming therefore that the Black Law was constitutional. Judge Eaton, in his charge to the jury, instructed them that "the law is constitutional and obligatory on the people of this State."

The jury deliberated for several hours, and returned to inform the Court that they could not agree. Twice more they were further instructed and sent out. Finally they told the

Court that there was no possibility that they could reach agreement. Seven were firm for conviction; five, for acquittal. This automatically meant a continuation of the case at the next term of the County Court, which would fall in December.

[CHAPTER XI]

Conviction and Appeal

"It is now the white man's country"

THE PROSECUTION WAS UNWILLING TO WAIT FOR THE DECEM-
ber term of the County Court. In a move which took the defense by surprise, they opened a new prosecution on the third
of October, in the State Supreme Court, sitting in Brooklyn.
Presiding was Chief Justice Daggett, who, according to May,
"was known to be hostile to the colored people, and a strenuous
advocate of the Black Law." He was a former professor of
law at Yale and had been among the opponents of the proposed
Negro college in New Haven. May, having expected a December trial, was committed to lecture in Massachusetts and could
not be present in court. He advised Prudence's counsel, if a verdict were given against her, "to carry the cause up to the Court
of Errors."

I have thought it best in this chapter to let the reader
see for himself the intricacies, ramifications, rationalizations,
and assumptions which were part of the constitutional debate
in the second trial and subsequent appeal. These passages,
perhaps a bit dry and demanding, will show the position of
peoples of color—both black men and red men—more effec-
tively than if shortened and paraphrased beyond what is presented here, which is still only a small part of the trial tran-
scripts.

The evidence and arguments were essentially the same as before. Judge Daggett, in his charge to the jury, said in part:

The persons contemplated in this act are *not citizens* within the obvious meaning of that section of the constitution of the *United States,* which I have just read [*Art. 4, sec. 2.*]. Let me begin by putting this plain question. Are *slaves* citizens? At the adoption of the constitution of the *United States,* every state was a slave state. *Massachusetts* had begun the work of emancipation within her own borders. And *Connecticut,* as early as 1784, had also enacted laws making all those free at the age of 25, who might be born within the State, after that time. We all know, that slavery is recognized in that constitution; and it is the duty of this court to take that constitution as it is, for we have sworn to support it. Although the term "slavery" cannot be found written out in the constitution, yet no one can mistake the object of the 3d section of the 4th article: "No persons held to service or labour in one state, under the laws thereof, escaping into another, shall, in consequence of any law or regulation therein, be discharged from such service or labour, but shall be delivered, upon claim of the party to whom such service or labour may be due."

The 2d section of the 1st article, reads as follows:— "Representative and direct taxes, shall be apportioned among the several states which may be included in this Union, according to their respective numbers, which shall be determined by adding to the whole number of free persons, including those bound to service for a term of years, and excluding *Indians* not taxed, three fifth of *all other persons.*" The "other persons" are slaves, and they became the basis of representation, by adding them to the white population in that proportion. Then slaves were not considered citizens by the framers of the constitution.

A *citizen* means a *freeman.* By referring to Dr. *Webster,* one of the most learned men of this or any other country, we have the following definition of the term—"Citizen: 1. A

native of a city, or an inhabitant who enjoys the freedom
and privileges of the city in which he resides. 2. A townsman,
a man of trade, not a gentleman. 3. An inhabitant; a dweller
in any city, town or country. 5. In the *United States,* it means
a person, native or naturalized, who has the privilege of ex-
ercising the elective franchise, and of purchasing and holding
real estate." [The quotation from Noah Webster, a Hartford
man, involved a veiled private thrust, for Judge Daggett
must certainly have known that W. W. Ellsworth was married
to the lexicographer's daughter Emily.]

Are *Indians* citizens? It is admitted in the argument that
they are not; but it is said, they belong to distinct tribes.
This cannot be true because all *Indians* do not belong to a
tribe. It may now be added, that by the declared law of *New
York, Indians* are not citizens; and the learned Chancellor
Kent, says "they never can be made citizens." *Indians* were
literally natives of our soil; they were born here; and yet
they are not citizens. . . .

Are *free blacks,* citizens? . . . I think Chancellor *Kent,*
whose authority it gives me pleasure to quote, determines
this question, by fair implication. Had this authority considered free blacks citizens, he had an ample opportunity
to say so. But what he has said excludes that idea: "In
most of the *United States,* there is a distinction in respect
to political privileges, between free white persons and free
coloured persons of *African* blood; and in no part of the
country do the latter, in point of fact, participate equally
with the whites, in the exercise of civil and political rights.
The *African* race are essentially a degraded caste, of inferior
rank and condition in society. Marriages are forbidden between them and whites, in some of the states, and when
not absolutely contrary to law, they are revolting, and regarded as an offence against public decorum. . . ."

To my mind, it would be a perversion of terms, and the
well known rule of construction, to say, that slaves, free
blacks, or *Indians,* were citizens, within the meaning of that
term, as used in the constitution. God forbid that I should

add to the degradation of this race of men; but I am bound by my duty, to say, they are not citizens.

I have thus shown you that this law is not contrary to the 2d section of the 4th art. of the constitution of the *United States;* for that embraces only citizens.

This time, the prosecution prevailed; the jury returned a verdict of guilty. Prudence's lawyers immediately filed a motion in arrest of judgment, on two technical points: that the superior court had not jurisdiction of the offenses charged; and that the "information" (that is, the particulars of the formal charge) was insufficient.

In July, 1834, the case was heard in the Supreme Court of Errors of the State of Connecticut, in Hartford, this time technically a proceeding of "Crandall *against* The State of Connecticut: in Error." The arguments of counsel on both sides were more clearly than ever focused on issues which reached beyond Canterbury, involving the moral dilemma of a nation moving slowly but inexorably toward the tragic purgation of fire and sword. They demand to be quoted at length, for they exhibit aspects of the attitudes toward race and color, in the early history of the nation, forgotten by or unknown to most people today. The contrast of acceptable attitudes between then and today is not the contrast between villainy and virtue, nor the grounds for some neurotic guilt, but is a contrast in moral sensitivity in different eras. As so often in history, and as it will be in the future many times, the views of what were then a handful of so-called visionaries or radicals find general acceptance now.

Prudence's counsel argued in part:

1. That the coloured persons mentioned in the information are *citizens* of their respective states. If they were white it is conceded they would be. The point turns, then, upon a distinction in *colour* only. This distinction, as the basis of fundamental rights, is, in the first place, novel. It is not recog-

nized, by the common law of *England*, or the principles of the *British* constitution; by our own declaration of independence; or by the constitution of Connecticut.

Secondly, it would be extremely inconvenient, if not impracticable, in its application. Who can tell the proportions and trace the mixtures of blood: What shall be the scale for the ascertainment of citizenship? Shall one half, one quarter, one twentieth, or the least possible taint of negro blood, be sufficient to take from its possessor the citizen character?

They then discussed the questions of birth, natural allegiance, the right of movement from state to state with the implied rights of education and other activities, the right to vote as a test of citizenship (it was pointed out that women could not vote but were none the less citizens).

Andrew Judson and C. F. Cleveland (the latter had studied law with Daniel Frost, of Canterbury, and was a member of the General Assembly, and later governor) began their argument with a comment, now ironic, upon the "magnitude of the question, as affecting not the town of *Canterbury* alone, but every town in the state and every state in the *Union;* as the principles urged by the counsel for the plaintiff in error, if established, would, in their consequences, destroy the government itself and this *American* nation—blotting out this nation of white men and substituting one from the *African* race—thus involving the honour of the state, the dignity of the people and the preservation of its name."

The crux of their argument was the meaning of the constitution with respect to people of color:

What *was* the *intention* of those who framed the constitution? Did they mean to place persons of colour on the footing of equality with themselves, and did they mean to make them *citizens?*

In answering this question, it matters little what may be the opinion of a few madmen or enthusiasts now, but what was the intention of the people of the *United States, at the time* when the constitution was adopted. . . .

We must now advert to the condition of the country, and the circumstances of the human race, then upon the face of this country. The white men and the coloured men composed the grand divisions of the human family. The *white* men then were entitled to particular privileges, above the coloured men: civil and political rights belonged, by the laws of all the states, to the former, but not to the latter. The coloured men were either natives, called *Indians,* or of *African* descent, called *Negroes.* From the *Indians* this whole country had but recently been conquered; and as in many of the states, they were still very numerous, it cannot even be pretended, that *Indians* were embraced in the term *citizen.* The *African* race, as a body, were then *slaves,* and held in bondage, by those who made the constitution. It was then deemed fit and proper to hold slaves. All the states in the Union were slave states, and their laws tolerated slavery. *Massachusetts* and *Connecticut* had passed laws that coloured persons born after a certain period should be free at 25, but they still held slaves. And can it be entertained for one moment, that those who framed the constitution should hold one portion of *a race of men* in bondage, while the other portion were made *citizens?* This would be strange inconsistency. Go back to the time when the constitution was made, and enquire after the condition of the country, and take into consideration all its circumstances, and all difficulties will be out of the way. *Then* it was not immoral to hold slaves. The *best men* bought and sold negroes, without a scruple. This impulse is of modern date; and however creditable to the heart, cannot alter the *constitution.* The immortal *Washington,* who presided at the convention, and who subscribed the instrument, under the laws of *Virginia* held more than one hundred slaves, as his property, on that day; and he was not thus inconsistent. He never intended to have you say, that the portion of the human race which were held in bondage were slaves, and the residue of that same colour were *citizens.* . . .

C. C. Burleigh.

C. C. BURLEIGH. Daguerreotype portrait, ca. 1845. Reproduced from *William Lloyd Garrison, 1805-1879: The Story of His Life Told by His Children.*

PRUDENCE CRANDALL PHILLEO in old age. Engraved from a
photograph, 1882. Reproduced from *The Century Magazine*,
October 1885.

The counsel for the plaintiff in error insist, "that the *distinction of colour is novel, inconvenient and impracticable.*" The position thus assumed will embrace *Indians,* and if we add to this another proposition laid down in the defence, that *birth* and not *colour* constitutes citizenship, the *Indians* are surely embraced. Can it be seriously contended, that the constitution does secure to *Indians* the right of citizens? Practically, it has never been so. When the constitution was adopted, this country had but recently emerged from the *Indian* wars. These wars were wars of conquest; and the white man had driven the red men from their lands, and acquired a title to those lands, by conquest and by force; and do you believe, that so soon, these conquered individuals would all be made *citizens?* There is another fact, which would repel this idea. In several of the states, when the constitution was adopted, there were more *Indians* than *white men;* and if citizens, the *Indians* would have had the supremacy. *Connecticut* has ever had within its limits numerous *Indians,* both tribes, and others not belonging to tribes; and whoever saw one of these *Indians* under our own laws, before or since the revolution, enjoying *one civil* or *political* privilege? If citizenship be a matter of favour, then surely the *Indian* stands far above the *African.* This is the *Indian's* home—it was once his soil, but it has passed into other hands. It is now the white man's country; and the white man is an *American* citizen. . . .

The distinction of colour, so far from being novel, is marked, in numerous ways, in our political system. . . .

The first law regarding naturalization was passed by Congress in 1790, and in it this precise and technical language is used: "Any alien, being a *free white person,* may become a *citizen,* by complying with the requisites hereinafter named." . . . Chancellor *Kent* settles this question beyond cavil: "The act of Congress confines the description of aliens capable of naturalization to 'free white persons.' I presume that this excludes the inhabitants of *Africa* and their descendants; and it may become a question, to what extent persons of mixed blood, as mulattoes, are excluded, and what shades or degrees of mixture of colour disqualify an alien from application for the benefits of the act of naturalization. Perhaps there might be difficulties as to the copper-coloured natives of *America,* or the yellow or tawny race of *Asiatics,* though I should doubt whether any of those were 'white persons,' within the purview of the law."

Thus the major argument went. Judson and Cleveland developed further points concerning the right of the state to regulate education, and its right to control the influx of outside persons, especially so-called undesirables or potential paupers. (This has become a live issue in recent times in the matter of the right of the poor to move from one state to another offering more generous welfare provisions.)

Judge Williams, in his opinion, conceded the paramount importance of the constitutional questions:

When the nature and importance of these questions are considered, the difficulties actually attending the construction of this clause of the constitution, the magnitude of the interests at stake, the excitement which always attends the agitation of questions connected with the interests of one class, and the liberties of another, more particularly at the present time; the jealousies existing on the one hand, and the expectations excited on the other; no desire is felt to agitate the subject unnecessarily.

This was his fainthearted preamble to evading the issue. Anticlimactically, he declined to offer an opinion at all on the question of principle, on the grounds of a "fatal defect" in the information, or charge, against Prudence. The Black Law, he held, was applicable only to unlicensed schools. The complaint against Prudence neglected to state that her school was not licensed. Therefore her conviction was found to be in error and the case was thrown out. Associate judges Bissell and

Church concurred; Chief Justice Daggett, who had presided over the second trial, dissented.

Prudence's supporters felt keen frustration at the evasion of the constitutional question. The issue of whether or not free black men could be citizens continued to haunt the country. In the Dred Scott case, of 1857, Chief Justice Roger Taney of the United States Supreme Court asserted that a Negro could not be a citizen. That case newly inflamed opinion and speeded the rush toward civil war. Daggett's ruling that free Negroes were not citizens was a precedent cited in the Dred Scott case.

Prudence's opponents felt only chagrin that they had failed to close her school in the courts. But they did not rest with that.

CHAPTER XII

Terror in
Canterbury

THE CANTERBURY SCHOOL WENT ON, AND SO DID THE UN-
abated resentment against it. Abroad, however, both in the
special meaning of the people of Canterbury as any place a
half-mile out of town, and also in the more common usage,
encouragement and honors came to Prudence.

In Boston, she was feted at banquets by Abolitionists and
colored organizations. Samuel May commissioned her portrait
in oils by the painter Francis Alexander. He retained it as a
prized possession until his old age. On the very afternoon of
his death, in 1871, he made a gift of the picture to Cornell University upon the condition, expressed to his old friend Andrew
Dixon White, its president, that women be admitted to the
university. It was a course to which White and others were
already committed and the first young woman had been en-
rolled the previous year.

From overseas and from Canada, a flow of letters, gifts,
and journalistic praises came to Prudence. *The Liberator*
printed letters of support and admiration from London, Glas-
gow, Edinburgh, and Bath. The Scottish ladies, in particular,
had sent over to Prudence, in the care of a travelling colleague
of Garrison's, a fine silver salver, engraved with a flowery
testimonial, many "elegant books," and other tokens of regard.
An Englishman named Edward S. Abdy published a book about
his journeys in America in which he mentioned making a side

trip from Providence to Canterbury for a visit to Prudence. "My object in thus going out of my road was to see what could have caused so much ire to the liberal minds of republican America." She had become a national, even international, figure on a minor scale.

For a time the school enjoyed that peculiar high morale that stems from a conviction of righteousness in the face of persecution. The students and faculty both worked devotedly. William H. Burleigh and Almira Crandall, both of whom taught there, reported that these besieged colored girls "made as good if not better progress than the same number of whites taken from the same position of life." The authentic eagerness to learn was dominant.

In their gala days, or exhibition sessions, the students took note of their special status. Once, in what was billed for its audience of friends and patrons as a "Mental Feast," four small girls in white dresses sang the following song composed by one of their teachers—whether by Prudence herself or another is not known. It might almost be sung to the tune of "Three little maids who all unwary, Come from a ladies' seminary," from *The Mikado*.

> Four little children here you see,
>   In modest dress appear;
> Come, listen to our song so sweet,
>   And our complaints you'll hear.
>
> 'Tis here we come to learn to read,
>   And write and cipher too;
> But some in this enlightened land
>   Declare 'twill never do.
>
> The morals of this favored town,
>   Will be corrupted soon.
> Therefore they strive with all their might,
>   To drive us to our homes.

Sometimes when we have walked the streets
   Saluted we have been,
By guns, and drums, and cow-bells too,
   And horns of polished tin.

With warnings, threats and words severe
   They visit us at times,
And gladly would they send us off
   To Afric's burning climes.

Our teacher too they put in jail,
   Fast held by bars and locks!
Did e'er such persecution reign
   Since Paul was in the stocks?

But we forgive, forgive the men,
   That persecute us so.
May God in mercy save their souls
   From everlasting wo!

But the town had not finished with the school. Hostility smouldered in Canterbury and burst into flame—literally. In the predawn hours, one morning, Prudence and some of her residents smelled smoke. They could not locate its source immediately, but some time after daylight an eruption of flame revealed it. The fire was quenched quickly. It was found that the arsonist had stuffed combustible materials under a corner of the house. Luckily the wood above it was soft and damp with rot. The tinder did not produce immediate flame, but only the slow smouldering that was smelled. By the time that spread to the dry wood and flamed up, the inhabitants of the house were alert to their danger.

Some Canterburians cried that this was a phony act of provocation, instigated by Prudence herself as a pretext for closing the school and saving face. The Windham County historian reports: "A very respectable colored man from Norwich, who had been mending a clock in the room in which the fire broke out, was made the victim of popular vengeance. To his utter astonishment he was seized by a writ and brought before Judge Adams, and though the evidence against him was utterly trifling was committed for trial." He was acquitted.

Garrison, writing to his prospective father-in-law George Benson, recalled the scene on the day that Frederick Olney, the alleged provocateur, was tried: "Your house was then thronged with colored pupils from Miss Crandall's school, who were summoned as witnesses at Mr. Olney's trial, and who had no other place in Brooklyn 'where to lay their heads' than your hospitable dwelling. . . . Some families, under such circumstances, would have been thrown into utter confusion—and bustle, bustle, nothing but bustle, and running to and fro, would have been the consequence. I was forcibly struck by the quietude of spirit manifested by you all, and by that domestic order which reigned paramount." It was no wonder that Prudence called the Benson place "Friendship's Valley."

So far in Prudence's story, the hatred of her opponents had been counterbalanced only by those two aspects of love classically known as *agapé* and *philos,* in the general and brotherly love of the Abolitionists who, from conscience and good will, had rallied to her. Now Eros comes unexpectedly and quite mysteriously into the scene. Background information is frustratingly scanty. Something drew under Prudence's personal spell the Reverend Calvin Philleo, a Baptist minister, of Ithaca, New York.

It is possible that the Reverend Levi Kneeland, of Packerville, his co-religionist, brought him into the scene. However it came about, in September, 1834, around the fourth of the month, Prudence was married to Calvin Philleo, in Brooklyn, Connecticut. One may guess that May and Kneeland both had parts in the ceremony. The bridal couple did not take a wedding trip, for the school was in session.

During the night of the ninth of September, a group of

men, identities unknown, stealthily surrounded the school in Canterbury, carrying clubs and iron bars. In concerted attack, they beat furiously at the house, making a fearful racket, scarring the white walls, bursting open the doors, destroying five window sashes, and shattering ninety panes of glass.

Samuel May was sent for. He arrived to find the morale of Prudence and her pupils also shattered at last, in the litter of this vandalism. He wrote: "Never before had Miss Crandall seemed to quail, and some of her pupils were afraid to remain another night under her roof."

The Liberator later printed a short essay "by one of Miss Crandall's juvenile pupils, in reference to the abandonment of her interesting school." The girl is not identified.

THE SEPARATION

It was one of the pleasant sunny mornings of September, when I took leave of my teacher and school-mates. Never, no, never, while memory retains a seat in my breast, shall I forget that trying hour. On the night preceding my departure, while all within was silent as the chamber of death, we were suddenly aroused by a tremendous noise; when, to our surprise, we found that a band of cruel men had rendered our dwelling almost untenantable. The next morning we were informed by our teacher, that the school would be suspended for the day, that he was going to a neighboring town to see a friend of ours: he accordingly went. [The teacher was William H. Burleigh; the friend, May.] In the afternoon he returned, accompanied by our friend, who requested that we might be called together. He, with feelings of apparent deep regret, told us we had better go to our homes. With regret I prepared to leave that pleasant, yet persecuted dwelling, and also my dear school-mates, in whose society I had spent so many hours; thankful to my heavenly Parent, that our lot was no worse; yet not without many tears did I return to my distant, solitary home. . . .

I could but acknowledge the probability of not meeting again in company with my school-mates. . . .

My teacher was ever kind: with him I saw religion, not merely adopted as an empty form, but a living, all-pervading principle of action. He lived like those who seek a better country: nor was his family devotion a cold pile of hypocrisy, on which the fire of God never descends.

Calvin Philleo strongly insisted that Prudence give up the school, perhaps wisely, though apparently he was not a fighter. She was ready to agree. The school ceased to be, amid the wreckage left from violent malice and lawlessness. Samuel May spoke its epitaph: "I felt ashamed of Canterbury, ashamed of Connecticut, ashamed of my country, ashamed of my color."

In the immediate wake of Prudence's defeat there were a number of ominous outbreaks of violent anti-black sentiments in Connecticut, as if an infection were spreading. In that same year, an anti-slavery Presbyterian minister was driven out of his church and out of Norwich. The next year or so saw anti-black mob actions by men called "worse than southern bloodhounds" in cities and towns including Hartford, Middletown, Meriden, Torrington, New Haven, New Canaan, and Norwalk. But a change of spirit was to come.

CHAPTER XIII

Aftermaths

THUCYDIDES, IN HIS DESCRIPTION OF THE DISAGREEMENTS BE-
tween Athens and the little island of Melos, during the jockey-
ing for allegiances in the Peloponnesian War, tells how the
Athenians, enraged by persistent Melian neutrality, sent a
fleet to lay waste the place. Not long after that punitive force
had sailed, the Athenians suffered a revulsion of conscience at
what they had done. Messengers were sent to try to overtake
and call back that vengeful expedition. But the fleet had passed
Fail-Safe and was not stopped in time.

The people of Canterbury were more fortunate. What
they had done was less drastic and was not fatal. All the same,
it is heartening to know that in due time, after Prudence was
gone, after her house was once more back in unobtrusive private hands and the black threat was lifted from Canterbury
Green, that town, and the County of Windham, and the State
of Connecticut, suffered a revulsion of conscience at what they
had done. Ellen Larned, the nineteenth-century historian of the
county, so often cited here, observed: "Miss Crandall did not
succeed in teaching many colored girls but she *educated* the
people of Windham County." The antislavery movement
flourished in the state. Antislavery societies claimed that some
persons who had opposed Prudence later became active Abolitionists. Philip Pearl, who as committee chairman had signed
the legislative report proposing the passage of the Black Law,
said some years later: "I could weep tears of blood for the

part I took in that matter. I now regard the law as utterly abominable." He took a vigorous role in achieving the repeal of that law in 1838. From that time up to, through, and after the Civil War, Connecticut fairly well earned the reputation for humane liberalism on which it had prided itself prematurely. Windham County was a leader in such causes. All of this cannot be attributed to reactions to Prudence's case, but it was certainly a factor along with the other anti-black incidents that followed close upon it. It was the incident which, for many men and women, forced an examination of conscience.

Judge Daggett's ruling that free Negroes were not citizens helped to thrust that issue before the nation. Connecticut supported and quickly ratified the fourteenth Constitutional amendment of 1868, by which the full rights of citizenship were affirmed for Negroes—though even in our time, the struggle to realize those rights in practice is still in progress with renewed and sometimes revolutionary intensity.

There are interesting aftermaths for some persons involved in Prudence's case. Andrew T. Judson, always the prime mover and most powerful force against her, continued to rise in public prominence, and there is no doubt that the public mood at the time of the Canterbury struggle helped his advancement.

There is one highly odd, and on any available evidence inexplicable, occurrence involving Andrew T. Judson and another Crandall from Canterbury. In 1836, Prudence's younger brother Reuben, a doctor of medicine, was arrested in Georgetown, District of Columbia, where he had established practice, and was confined for nearly a year in "a noisome jail," and subsequently tried, charged with "publishing" seditious libels and inciting to seditious acts. This was for having in his possession, and allegedly circulating, various pamphlets of the American Anti-Slavery Society. This makes him sound like a true kinsman of Prudence. Yet among the character witnesses called on behalf of Reuben Crandall was the Honorable A. T.

Judson, then serving in the House of Representatives. Here are some passages from Judson's brief testimony, from the published report of the trial:

> I have known Dr. Crandall from his early boyhood. I am a Representative from the district in which he was born. His father lives in the town where I live, in my immediate neighborhood. He studied with my family physician, Dr. Harris; and I have been acquainted with his reputation. No young man stood better in society. . . . Dr. Crandall is the brother of Prudence Crandall. In the winter of 1833, Prudence Crandall, having kept a school for young ladies, immediately changed it, at the instigation of Garrison and others, to a colored school. It was the object of Tappan and Garrison to get colored children from the south and educate them and send them back. I had received a petition, being then a representative, for the legislature to interfere and suppress it by law. I had been to New York, and was going home in the steamboat, when I saw Dr. Crandall.

Here an objection was raised to his repeating conversation, but the judge overruled it. Judson continued:

> I told him the difficulty we had had with his sister. He said he was going to break up the school. He said he didn't know as he could, because Prudence was a very obstinate girl; but he had another sister, younger, then engaged in it, that he could at all events get her away. I told him, that in a few days I was going to present the *projet* of a law, and if he was going on for that purpose I would aid him. When we arrived at Norwich, the stage was full, and I took him in my gig, and carried him home. I always understood he used his whole influence to break up the school as much as any other individual, and appeared to be as zealous to effect that object. I have not seen him since till I saw him here in jail.

Reuben Crandall was acquitted of the charges, though his
health was said to have been severely damaged by his sojourn
in jail. He died some two years later, and various passing allu-
sions in Abolitionist writings list him with the righteous, like
his sister. But what a peculiar box that incident opens up! I
cannot explain it. That is the beginning and end of it. Nowhere in the known chronicles of the Prudence Crandall case
does the name of her brother Reuben occur. Nowhere is there
a hint of his opposition to her school, or of an attempt by him
to dissuade Almira from her part in it. That remains a mystery,
along with the curious matter of Reuben's arrest and trial
in Washington over the antislavery pamphlets. What was he
doing with those, anyway, if Andrew T. Judson was willing to
serve as a character witness for him and Dr. Crandall was
willing to accept that testimony?

Destiny yet held an ironic task in reserve for Andrew T.
Judson. Some eight years after the clash with Prudence Crandall, Judson, as a judge of the United States District Court,
was one of several judges required at various times to rule on
the *Amistad* slave case, which agitated the nation and brought
Judson under direct pressure from a President of the United
States.

In 1838 there occurred a mutiny of some fifty or more
slaves, recently captured in Africa and being reshipped from
Cuba aboard the Spanish schooner *Amistad*. Though the slave
trade was already outlawed by most European nations and the
United States, Havana remained a center of what was left
of the ugly business. The mutinous slaves compelled the rem-
nant of the Spanish crew to sail north. The ship was taken
into custody by a United States warship off Long Island, and
the slaves were brought ashore in Connecticut, at New Haven,
which became the first seat of the complex legal and diplomatic controversy over them. The owners of the vessel and of
the slaves—a variety of interested parties, not United States

citizens—sued for recovery of the *Amistad* and also of the slaves—both as property, and on charges of mutiny and murder.

Antislavery people rallied to the defense of the *Amistad* blacks, a remarkably dignified, impressive group whose story is worth reading at length. They caught the imaginations of many people. Particularly fascinating was the imposing figure of their leader, Cinqué, "A man of giant frame . . . a lion bound," as William Cullen Bryant described him in his poem "The African Chief." Among those who interceded for them were our old friend Arthur Tappan, now a New Haven resident, and his brother Lewis.

The case became extraordinarily complex in its legal and diplomatic entanglements, which we cannot pursue here. It fell to Judson to go on board the U. S. S. *Washington,* at New Haven, to see the slaves and some of the claimants, and to hear preliminary testimony. He is reported by some chronicles to have been ill-disposed toward the blacks and consequently inclined to sympathy with the claimants. In any case, he determined that the case must go before the United States Circuit Court, at Hartford. Meanwhile, the Spanish government, at the highest level, had communicated to the United States its wish to have the Africans surrendered to it, to be tried in Spanish courts. This the administration of President Martin Van Buren was inclined to do; and this the Abolitionists were determined to prevent.

The pro-Spanish faction argued that Judson had been wrong to proclaim any sort of jurisdiction by United States courts, that the whole case should have been a matter of negotiation between the governments of the United States and of Spain, looking toward the surrender of the ship and the blacks to the Spanish. Pressure was put upon Judson to reverse himself and deny the court's jurisdiction.

Judson refused. He had made a decision; he stuck by it. Meanwhile, a formidable champion of justice, old John Quincy

Adams, had been drawn into the defense of the Africans. He was a foe of slavery though not a radical Abolitionist. The former President, seventy-three years old and the most distinguished member of the House of Representatives, openly criticized the Administration for attempting to put political pressure on the courts.

Judson, who was in the anomalous position of being pro-Administration and at least previously anti-black in sentiment, was not involved when the case first was heard in the Circuit Court, but it was referred back to his hands, in the District Court, for the complicated debate over jurisdiction. Judson delayed his decision, a delay personally vexing to President Van Buren, who wanted the matter dismissed from the courts and left for his Administration to settle on the diplomatic level. That would unquestionably doom the blacks to a return to slavery and probable execution.

At last, in January of 1840, Judson delivered his decision that "The District Court of Connecticut has jurisdiction." and directed that "these Africans be delivered to the President of the United States under the law of 1818 to be transported to Africa, there to be delivered to the agency appointed to receive them and conduct them home."

This was not the form of delivery to the President that the President had wanted. The Africans were to be freed and sent home, over Spanish, and some American, protest. Judson had followed his judicial conscience against heavy pressure from the White House and at the risk of his own possible political future. It was hard to know who was the more amazed, his friends or the Abolitionists. The government appealed against his decision to the Supreme Court. The Africans were represented there by John Quincy Adams himself, early in 1841. "Old Man Eloquent," in his argument, sternly denounced and submitted "to the censure of this Court the form and manner of proceedings of the Executive in this case." A former President was challenging before the Supreme Court the conduct of one of his successors. In two dramatic sessions Adams swayed the Court. Judge Andrew T. Judson's decision was upheld. The *Amistad* slaves were freed and sent home to Africa.

CHAPTER XIV

Prudence's
Last Years

WHEN THE SCHOOL CLOSED, IN THAT CLIMACTIC SEPTEM-
ber of 1834, the Reverend Calvin Philleo took his bride back to
Ithaca. Connecticut would see her no more, but it would not
forget her. The once lovely house, the cost of restoring which
was one factor in the decision to give up the school, was sold
and in time made lovely again. Prudence's brother Hezekiah
went west with the Philleos. From New York State they went
on to Illinois, where Calvin Philleo died in 1874. Prudence and
Hezekiah moved on to Kansas, where they settled in Elk Falls,
a town somewhere in the range of a hundred miles south of
Emporia, but too small, if it survives, to appear on a modern
roadmap atlas. There Hezekiah died.

In 1886 a move was started, in Canterbury, to grant Prudence a pension, in absentia, as compensation for the wrongs
she had undergone some five decades past; an active party
in this effort was no less a person than Andrew Judson Clark,
a nephew of her old adversary.

The petition of the people of Canterbury, filed in the
State archives as House Petition No. 48, January Session, 1886,
may be seen in a photostatic copy in the State Library in Hartford, written in the copperplate script of the era.

> *To the Honorable, the Senate and House of Representa-
> tives,* in General Assembly Convened;
> We, the Undersigned, Citizens of the State, and of the

Town of Canterbury, mindful of the dark blot that rests upon our fair fame and name, for the cruel outrages inflicted upon a former citizen of our Commonwealth, a noble Christian Woman (Miss Prudence Crandall, now Mrs. Philleo) at present in straightned circumstances, and far advanced in years, respectfully pray your Honorable Body to make such late reparation for the wrong done her, as your united wisdom, your love of justice, and an honorable pride in the good name of our noble State, shall dictate.

It will be remembered that she stands in the Records of the Court as a convicted criminal for the offence of teaching colored girls to read, and suffered unnumbered outrages in person and property, for a benevolent work, that now to its great honor, the General Government itself is engaged in.

We respectfully suggest that you make a fair appropriation in her behalf, which shall at once relieve her from any anxiety for the future, and from the official stigma that rests upon her name, and purge our own record from its last remaining stain, in connection with the colored race.

And your petitioners will ever pray.

It bears 112 signatures.

The State Legislature finally granted her an annuity of $400—an unusual if not a unique action. There had even been talk of giving her back her house. Prudence, then eighty-two, wrote that she did not want it, being quite content in her "little pioneer box house of three rooms." She accepted the annuity, not as charity—she would "rather dig than beg"—but as the settlement of a "just debt" for the destruction of her "hopes and prospects." Most of all, she was happy at "the change that has been wrought in the views and feelings of the mass of the people."

An engaging man, George B. Thayer, has given us the most vividly living, breathing portrait of Prudence to be found anywhere. It also bears out, in her own words, my belief that despite, or because of, her virtues she was also a difficult person, even as a minister's wife.

Thayer was a Hartford journalist and bicycle buff, a member of the Connecticut Bicycle Club, who must have brought more glory to it than any other member. Setting forth from Hartford in April, 1886, on one of the old bicycles with the immense front wheel and the tiny rear one, he rode some eleven thousand miles, from Hartford to San Francisco and back, with all sorts of meanderings on the way. He financed the adventure by sending back letters to the Hartford *Evening Post,* which in 1887 were published in a now obscure, rare, and pleasing little book: *Pedal and Path; Across the Continent Awheel and Afoot.*

The frontispiece shows the doughty Thayer, clad in knickerbockers and a fatigue cap, a pack on his back, standing with his bicycle, its great front wheel nearly as tall as he is. His lightly bearded face is set in an appropriate look of pioneer determination and dauntlessness. His twenty-third chapter is "A Visit to Prudence Crandall," whom he calls of "almost national renown." Let him report its high lights himself.

The country south of Emporia, for eighty or ninety miles, is a gentle rolling prairie, which looks as fresh and green as in the spring, and the timber and numerous farm-houses tend to break up what little monotony there is in the prospect. But all the enjoyment of the trip was soon swept away by a drizzling rain which set in on the second day of the ride, and I was glad to find even a grassy place on the side of the road to walk on, for in the road the sticky black clay would clog up under the saddle and entirely stop the wheel. However, after pushing the machine along in this manner for eighteen or twenty miles, I was made glad by the sight of Elk Falls, a town of seven or eight hundred inhabitants, situated within thirty miles of the northern border of the Indian "Nation." . . .

Inquiring at the first house I came to, the man said, pointing to a house west of us on the brow of a hill, "Mrs. Philleo lives out on that farm, about a mile and a half from town. A Mr. Williams lives with her and takes care of the farm, but she goes around lecturing some, talking on temperance, spiritualism, and so on."

It turned out that Prudence had quite recently bought a place in town next to the Methodist Church. Thayer arrived there.

I was pleasantly received by Mr. Williams, a man of 35, with brown hair and mustache, large blue eyes, and a most sympathetic, almost affectionate, manner. "Mrs. Philleo," he explained, "is at church. She enjoys excellent health, and it is wonderful how much she, a woman of 84 years, can endure. Yesterday she wanted to ride over to the farm and see about some thing, and before I was ready to come home she started on foot and got clear home before I overtook her, and she didn't seem tired either." Just then Mrs. Philleo came in, and said cordially, "I am glad to see any one from good old Connecticut." As she removed her bonnet, it showed a good growth of sandy gray hair, smoothed back with a common round comb, and cut straight around, the ends curling around in under and in front of her ears; of medium height, but somewhat bent and spare, and with blue eyes and a face very wrinkled, and rather long; her chin quite prominent, and a solitary tooth on her upper jaw, the only one seen in her mouth.

She smiled with her eyes, and with a pleasant voice, said: "Come, you must be hungry, coming so far" (I had only told her then I came from Connecticut on the bicycle), and she urged the apple pie, ginger snaps, johnny-cakes, potatoes, ham, bread and butter, and tea, upon me promiscuously, and in great profusion. "No, as my grandmother used to say, I never break a cup, you must take another full one. Now do you make yourself at home; I know you must be tired. Why, you have seen enough to write a book. . . . Now come into the other room; I want to show you some pictures."

So, talking every minute, we went into the sitting room, and drawing up rocking-chairs, we sat down cosily together. "I am going to have these photographs of these noble men all put into a frame together. I don't want them in an album, for I have to turn and turn the leaves so much. I want them in a frame, so I can get the inspiration from them at a glance. This is Samuel Coit, who did so much last winter in my behalf, and this is S. A. Hubbard of the [Hartford] *Courant*. This is——. Why I see you know all of these noble souls. Well, I want to read you a letter he sent me," and she slowly picked out the words of the writer who said, among other generous things, that he would be only too glad to load her down with any number of his books, and would send her a complete file of them. The letter was signed Samuel L. Clemens.

"But," she added, "he has never sent them. Probably so busy he forgot it. I do wish I could see them, for I had a chance once to read part of 'Innocents Abroad,' and I do like his beautiful style of expression. And here is Major Kinney, and George C. Sumner, and Rev. Mr. Twichell. What grand good men they are. And this—you say you have heard him preach! How much I would give to hear that great soul speak," and she handed me Rev. Mr. Kimball's* photograph. . . . In this collection also, were photographs of William Lloyd Garrison, Wendell Phillips, and other anti-slavery friends of hers, and I noticed several others of Garrison framed and hung about the house. When I expressed the opinion that the amount of her pension was too small in proportion to the injury inflicted, she said: "Oh, I am so thankful for that. It is so much better than nothing."

The next day:

After breakfast, I sat down to glance through a book I had seen her reading, "Is Darwin Right?," by William Den-

---

* Author of one of the earliest retrospective accounts of Prudence's case, "Connecticut's Canterbury Tale," a pamphlet of 1886, in support of the move to grant Prudence a pension.

ton of Massachusetts. Soon she came into the sitting-room with a pan of apples, and drawing a low rocking-chair up in front of me said, "Now you must stop reading, for I want to talk," and we talked. In fact, she became so interested in the conversation, and so far forgot herself that, in cutting out the worm-holes from the apples, she once put the worthless portion into her mouth and munched it thoroughly before she discovered her mistake. The conversation drifted from one subject to another, and on her part it was carried on in a clear, connected, and enlightened manner.

I can only give a few sentences of hers. "My whole life has been one of opposition. I never could find any one near me to agree with me. Even my husband opposed me, more than anyone. He would not let me read the books that he himself read, but I did read them. I read all sides, and searched for the truth whether it was in science, religion, or humanity. I sometimes think I would like to live somewhere else. Here, in Elk Falls, there is nothing for my soul to feed upon. Nothing, unless it comes from abroad in the shape of books, newspapers, and so on. There is no public library, and there are but one or two persons in the place that I can converse with profitably for any length of time. No one visits me, and I begin to think they are afraid of me. I think the ministers are afraid I shall upset their religious beliefs, and advise the members of their congregation not to call on me, but I don't care. I speak on spiritualism sometimes, but more on temperance, and am a self-appointed member of the International Arbitration League. I don't want to die yet. I want to live long enough to see some of these reforms consummated. I never had any children of my own to love, but I love every human being, and I want to do what I can for their good."

After dinner while I was reading—for there is a host of good books in the house—she sat down to copy off a short account of my trip I had written at her request the night before for a local paper, but every few minutes she would stop to talk on some subject that had just entered her mind, and sometimes we would both commence speaking at the same instant. "Go ahead," she would say, or "keep on, I have kept hold of that idea I had," pressing thumb and forefinger together, and then again she would say, "When you get another idea, just let it out." And so two days passed, very pleasantly, for me at least. There was no subject upon which I was conversant, but that she was competent to talk and even lead in the conversation, and she introduced many subjects to which I found I could only listen. At night Mr. Williams's bed and my own were in the same room, and this gave him an opportunity to say of Mrs. Philleo, "I never knew a person of a more even temperament. She is never low spirited, never greatly elated. When things don't go right she never frets." And of him, when he was off at work, she said, "You don't know how much comfort I get from my adopted son. We have lived together nearly four years, and my prayer is that he will grow up a noble man to do all the good he can in this world." . . . The last thing she said as I left them was, "if the people of Connecticut only knew how happy I am, and how thankful I am to them, it would make them happy too." . . .

The State of Connecticut certainly is to be congratulated that it did not neglect its opportunity last winter. What a shame had this good woman, this great mind, gone to another world without having even that slight justice done it. Very few people in Connecticut realize what a narrow escape they had from a lasting disgrace.

Prudence died on January 28, 1889, in Elk Falls, in her eighty-sixth year.

In March of 1834, William Lloyd Garrison had written and published in *The Liberator*

An Acrostic
Addressed to Her Who Is the Ornament of Her Sex

Proudly shall History upon its page
Record in living characters thy name,
Unequalled Woman in this servile age!

Dauntless, though wrapt in Persecution's flame!
E'en as a star shall thy example shine,
Nor Time's profoundest depths obscure its light;
Cheering Posterity's extended line;
Effulgent, fresh, and lovely to the sight.

Courageously pursue thy purpose high;
Reclaim from ignorance the darkened mind;
An outcast race around thee prostrate lie,
Naked and hungry, captive, sick and blind.
Dare still to be their guide—instructress—friend,
And bright shall be the crown of thy reward;
Let brutal men in wrath with thee contend—
Loved—honoured *thou* shalt be, and *they* abhorred.

Today it seems naive and overinflated, but it was the common laudatory style of its age. Prudence had earned the praise. Truly, she was not servile—nor content that any fellow man should live in servility.

Sources

Manuscripts

Connecticut State Library, Hartford. Material in Larned collection: four autograph letters of Prudence Crandall, clippings, and notes. Twelve items.

Connecticut State Library, Hartford. Writ of arrest of Prudence Crandall, June 27, 1833. Judgment binding her over to superior court, September 26, 1833. Two documents.

Connecticut State Library, Hartford. Petition of the citizens of the town of Canterbury, Conn., and others to the Connecticut General Assembly for aid for Miss Prudence Crandall. House Petition No. 48, January Session, 1886.

Government Publications

Public Statute Laws of the State of Connecticut. 1833. Chapter IX: The text of the "Black Law."

State Supreme Court, 10 Conn., 339. "Crandall *against* The State of Connecticut: In Error."
The official record of the trial on appeal.

Other Publications

Morris Bishop, *Early Cornell: 1865–1900.* Ithaca, N. Y.: Cornell University Press, 1962.

Alfred Thurston Child, Jr., "Prudence Crandall and the Canterbury Experiment." In *Bulletin of Friends' Historical Association,* Vol. 22, 1933.

Timothy Dwight, *Travels in New England and New York.* 4 vols.

Edited by B. M. Soloman. Cambridge, Mass.: Harvard University Press, 1969.

G. B. Emerson, S. May, and T. J. Mumford, *Memoir of Samuel Joseph May*. Boston: Roberts Brothers, 1873.

Edmund Fuller, "Prudence of Canterbury." In *The American Scholar*, Summer, 1949.

W. P. & F. J. Garrison, *William Lloyd Garrison, 1805-1879. The Story of His Life.* 4 vols. New York: The Century Co., 1885–1889. One of the indispensable sources.

John C. Kimball, *Connecticut's Canterbury Tale* (pamphlet). Hartford, Conn.: Plimpton Press, 1888. The first important retrospective account of the case, though it contains some inaccuracies.

Ellen D. Larned, *History of Windham County, Connecticut.* 2 vols. Worcester, Mass.: C. Hamilton, 1874–1880. One of the indispensable sources.

Samuel J. May, *Some Recollections of Our Anti-Slavery Conflict.* Boston: Fields, Osgood, 1869. One of the indispensable sources. A pamphlet, *Miss Prudence Crandall and the Canterbury School* is a reprint of a chapter from it.

————, *Two Letters of Samuel J. May.* Pamphlet. 1833. Open letters addressed to Andrew T. Judson, following the town meeting of Canterbury of March 9, 1833.

William A. Owens, *Black Mutiny: The Revolt on the Schooner Amistad.* Boston, Mass.: Pilgrim Press, 1968. Principal source for the discussion here of the *Amistad.* It is the source of the brief quotation from J. Q. Adams' argument before the Supreme Court.

Calvin W. Philleo, *Twice Married; A Story of Connecticut Life.* New York: Dix & Edwards, 1855. A work of sentimental fiction that describes the Canterbury region as it was in Prudence's time.

Muriel Rukeyser, *Willard Gibbs.* New York: Doubleday, Doran & Co., 1942. Contains a chapter on the *Amistad* case.

Edwin M. and Miriam R. Small, "Prudence Crandall, Champion of Negro Education." In *The New England Quarterly*, Vol. 17, 1944.

Horatio T. Strother, *The Underground Railroad in Connecticut.*
Middletown, Conn.: Wesleyan University Press, 1962.
Lewis Tappan, *The Life of Arthur Tappan.* New York: Hurd &
Houghton, 1870.
George B. Thayer, *Pedal and Path: Across the Continent Awheel
and Afoot.* Hartford, Conn.: Hartford Evening Post Associa-
tion, 1887. A unique and charming volume which gives the
only vivid, first-hand view of the personality and tempera-
ment of Prudence Crandall, in her old age, in Elk Falls,
Kansas.
Elizabeth Yates, *Prudence Crandall: Woman of Courage.* New
York: E. P. Dutton & Co., Inc., 1955. Fiction, for ages 10–
14. Oversimplified, overheroic, sentimental.

Periodicals and Unsigned Reports
The Liberator. Boston: Mass. Garrison & Knapp, 1831–1865.
The files of Garrison's famous journal, containing many refer-
ences to Prudence Crandall's case between February 20, 1833,
and the year 1840. The best guide is the marginal references
accompanying the discussion of Prudence in *William Lloyd
Garrison,* above.
*Report of the Arguments of Counsel in the Case of Prudence Cran-
dall.* By a member of the bar. Boston, Mass.: Garrison &
Knapp, 1834.
Statement of Facts. Brooklyn, Conn.: Advertiser Press, 1833.
Pamphlet setting forth the views of those opposed to Prudence
Crandall, immediately following her first trial.
The Trial of Reuben Crandall, M.D. By a member of the bar.
New York: H. R. Piercy, 1836.
The Unionist. Brooklyn, Conn. Issue of August 8, 1833, New
York Historical Society, New York, N. Y. Issue of September
5, 1833, American Antiquarian Society, Worcester, Mass.